WOMEN OF THE BIBLE.

Ruth Gleaning

AUBURN, N.Y.
DERBY, MILLER & C?

SEVENTH THOUSAND.

Historical and Descriptive Sketches

OF THE

WOMEN OF THE BIBLE

FROM

EVE OF THE OLD TO THE MARYS OF THE NEW TESTAMENT.

BY P. C. HEADLEY.

AUBURN:
DERBY, MILLER, AND COMPANY.
1851.

Entered according to Act of Congress, in the year 1850,
BY DERBY, MILLER, AND CO.
In the Clerk's Office of the Southern District of New York.

THOMAS B. SMITH, STEREOTYPER,
216 WILLIAM STREET, N. Y.

TO

IRENE,

MY ONLY AND BELOVED SISTER,

THIS VOLUME

Is Affectionately Inscribed.

It was not the design of adding essentially to Biblical Literature, neither the *cacoethes scribendi*, that induced the Author to increase the number of similar works which have appeared.

It was the suggestion of another, enforced by the consideration, that while there are elegant Gift Books of Female Scripture Biography, there is no volume of the kind for more general reading. The Bible is a book of facts, developing all the great principles of moral obligation which concern man. In these sketches it has been the steady aim to preserve those principles inviolate, and where imagination has aided in completing the narrative, as constantly to observe the known laws of human action, and their peculiar modification in the Hebrew commonwealth.

The sketch of "The Queen of Sheba," is from the pen of the REV. H. W. PARKER; and by permission a few extracts are taken from a recent work entitled, "Sacred Scenes and Characters."

The Frontispiece and tasteful illustrations are from Original Design, by the promising young Artist, C. L. DERBY.

The biographies are in chronological order, and will make an outline of Scripture History, including nearly all the heroic and distinguished women of the Sacred Annals.

The circumstances under which they were written will unavoidably leave traces of haste; but the volume is committed to the tide of popular favor, and will fulfil its mission if it breathe encouragement to the maternal heart, and infuse the spirit of their high destiny to any extent, into the minds of the women of America—a land, which in its moral, no less than its civil aspect, is the world's modern Palestine.

CONTENTS.

I.—EVE.

                                                                                                   PAGE

Adam alone in Paradise.—His first Interview with Eve.—Her Temptation and Fall.—Birth of Abel.—His Death.—The old Age and Last Hours of Eve 13

II.—SARAH.

Sarah's Youth and Marriage.—Life in Palestine.—Abram's Visit to the Court of Pharaoh.—She entertains Angels.—Hagar's Exile.—Birth of Isaac.—Hagar banished the second time.—Sacrifice of Isaac.—Sarah's Death and Burial 27

III.—REBEKAH.

The Embassy of Isaac to Haran.—Rebekah at the Well.—The Scene in the Domestic Circle.—Departure for Canaan.—Isaac walking in the Fields sees the Servant coming, and goes forth to meet his Bride.—Rebekah's Death.—Her Character 45

IV.—RACHEL.

Jacob's Journey to Haran.—Resting by the Well, Rachel comes with her Flock.—Makes himself known.—Serves Seven Years for her.—The Fraud of Laban compels him to take Leah, and render another Seven Years' Service for Rachel.—The Flight.—Her Death 65

CONTENTS.

V.—MIRIAM.

Miriam by the Nile.—Passage of the Red Sea, and her Song.—Her Fall.—Death and Burial.—Power of Faith **75**

VI.—DEBORAH.

Deborah beneath the Palm-tree at Bethel.—Her Interview with Barak.—The Summoning to Battle.—The Conflict and Victory.—Song of Deborah and Barak.—Her Character **91**

VII—JEPTHA'S DAUGHTER.

Jeptha in Exile.—Called to the Generalship of the Army.—His Vow.—The Victory and Return.—Met by his Daughter.—Her Lamentation and Sacrifice **105**

VIII.—DELILAH.

Life's Contrasts.—Samson's Love and Fall.—Scene from Samson Agonistes.—The Temple of Dagon overthrown.—Delilah Compared with the Hebrew Women **115**

IX.—RUTH.

The Design of her History.—The Trial in Moab.—Ruth and Naomi return to Bethlehem.—Ruth Gleaning in the Field of Boaz.—His Generosity.—Falls in Love with the beautiful Moabitess, and Marries her.—Her Character **127**

X.—HANNAH.

Her Trial and Faith.—The Annual Pilgrimage to Shiloh.—Her Prayer and the Answer.—Birth and Consecration of Samuel.—Maternal Influence **141**

XI.—QUEEN OF SHEBA.

Description of Arabia, the Queen's Realm.—Her Character.—Journey to Solomon's Court.—The Royal Interview.—Her Return.—Woman's Sphere **149**

XII.—JEZEBEL.

Jezebel's Marriage and Influence over the King.—Her Persecution of the Prophets.—She is unmoved by the Miracle on Mount Carmel.—The Murder of Naboth.—The Queen's Tragical Death.—Comparative Seclusion a Blessing to Woman.................................... 173

XIII.—ATHALIAH.

The Family of Ahab.—Athaliah Marries Prince Jehoram, and enters on her Career of Crime.—Massacre of the "Seed Royal," and Preservation of Joash.—The Revolution.—Athaliah Slain.—Origin of Monarchy... 187

XIV.—THE SHUNAMITE.

Internal Evidence of Inspiration of the Bible.—Shunem.—The Woman entertains Elisha.—Promise of a Son.—The Boy goes to the Harvest Fields, is smitten with Disease, borne to his Mother, and Dies at Noon.—The Shunamite hastens to the Mountain Home of Elisha.—He restores to her the Sleeper.................................... 195

XV.—ESTHER.

Vast Consequences from Small Events.—The Festival of Ahasuerus.—He commands the Queen to grace the Banquet with her Presence.—The Refusal and Divorce.—Esther's Appearance with the Beautiful Maidens in the King's Palace.—Haman's Plot, and Esther's Petition.—Her Success and Noble Character.................................... 209

XVI.—ELIZABETH.

The Promise of a Messiah.—Zacharias in the Temple.—Family Scenes.—Birth of John.—Maternal Influence upon the Baptist's Character... 229

XVII.—THE VIRGIN MARY.

Her Interview with the Angel.—Visit to Elizabeth.—Joseph's Trial.—The Sojourn at Bethlehem.—The Family keep the Passover at Jerusalem.—Their Residence in Nazareth.—The Marriage in Cana.—Scene at the Door of the Synagogue in Capernaum.—Mary at the Cross.—In the "Upper Room" at Jerusalem, after Christ's Ascension, with the Praying Disciples.................................... 239

XVIII.—THE SISTERS, MARTHA AND MARY.

PAGE

The Sisters, Martha and Mary.—Contrast between the Old and the New Dispensation.—The Family of Bethany.—Lazarus' Sickness and Death.—His Resurrection.—The Distinguishing Traits in the Characters of Martha and Mary.—The Saviour's Last Supper and Interview with them.. 261

XIX.—TABITHA, OR DORCAS.

Joppa.—Tabitha's Residence there, her Character, and Death.—She is Raised from the Dead by Peter.—Woman's Influence as a Maiden, Wife, and Mother.. 275

Eve has a brief biography in the Sacred Record. Without childhood or youth, she came from the moulding hand of her Creator, in the full maturity of her powers, and in the perfection of human beauty.

To Adam as he awakened from repose, she came like a morning vision—the bright presence of a celestial. How long he had been alone in Paradise, we do not know. But he had held communion with God and the angels; and given names to the varieties of animal creation, which passed before him in obedient homage to their solitary king. He had looked with rapture upon the high arch of his wide domain, with its wandering clouds and nightly stars—upon the flashing rivers, and waving foliage with its golden fruit.

The world of thought within, was pure and beautiful as the world without. Reason was unshaken in its majesty and clear in its judgment tone, conscience perpetually peaceful, and the heart tuned to the harmonies of Heaven. "He was great yet disconsolate" in his garden of manifold delights. He heard sometimes the voice of Jehovah, but it came to his listening ear with the authority of a Sovereign. The Seraphim walked with him in the groves of Eden, but they were of a higher and more etherial nature. Besides, they left him to many hours of solitude, in which no language of sympathy broke on his contemplations. Around him, in all the myriads of submissive creatures, he found in none the light of thought and the dignity of moral character. It is not strange with a *human soul*, if a shadow of mysterious loneliness at times passed over his ample brow. He longed for a being who could enter into the sphere of meditation and feeling peculiar to man. This, his only want, was gratified by the Deity, when he brought the first maiden and wife, in " unadorned beauty," to his beating heart. He received with joyful welcome his fair companion, and recognized the object of his social affections.

They flowed freely from their unsullied fountain, and were reciprocated with the confiding love of woman. She was his equal in origin and immortality; and they went forth from the marriage rite, which fell from the lips of God, to contemplate his works, and lift an anthem of praise—the first epithalamium of earth. To Adam, Paradise must have put on new glory, and the very trees seemed to toss their green crowns in gladness above his path.

He told Eve what God had done in fitting up their abode, and gave her the names of animals sporting by her side.

When he paused before the mystic "tree of the knowledge of good and evil," near which were the spreading and luxuriant branches of the "tree of life," he repeated the awful sanctions of eternal Law, which invested that single tree with fearful interest. It pointed like an index-finger to the skies, and reminded them of the holiness and authority of the Infinite Lawgiver. It was there, though one among thousands, in solitary and solemn sublimity, at once a memorial of love, a test of loyalty, and a beacon of warning, bidding them beware how they dashed madly down the precipice of moral ruin. They contemplated that forbidden object silently, until they bowed and prayed for strength to walk in obedience, erecting beneath its shade a family altar to the Lord.

Beautiful scene! Heaven bent lovingly over it, and

>————"Aside the Devil turned,
>For envy."

So time passed on, with no chronometer but the joy of holy affection—with no dial but the shadows of evening that brought no gloom, and the dawn of morning that revealed more of the glorious Giver, and added new notes of praise to their hymns of worship.

But one day Eve wandered alone amid the bowers of the garden, and the fallen Archangel watched her goings and plotted her ruin. He understood the subtle power of influence wielded with the magic of genius, and approached her with a question touching the possibility that Jehovah *could* with propriety prohibit any pleasurable indulgence. The purity of Eve's mind was stained by *indecision;* she did not repel the insinuation and affirm the justness of the interdiction.

The tempter became more positive, and assured her that she might partake of the fruit without apprehension of the threatened death, and would besides, attain a glorious pre-eminence in knowledge. She listened, and cast a glance of desire upon the pendent boughs, whose fragrant harvest seemed to invite her touch. Fatal pause! the first act in a moral revolution, extending over the ages of time and the cycles of eternity.

"Forth reaching to the fruit, she plucked, she ate."

Could she then have looked down the

stream of history, and read all the tragedies that moment of pleasure was preparing for the souls of her offspring, how would her heart have burst with agony, and tears of blood have stained that cheek, flushed with the excitement of the conflict with conscience, and the enjoyment of her unconscious fall. Pleased with the achievement, and meeting not immediately the mysterious doom she had feared, Eve sought the bower of Adam, and urged him to eat of the pleasant fruit; for it was truly as the serpent had said. He, too, fell before the temptation presented in two-fold strength, and the victory of "the powers of darkness" was complete.

A long and exultant shout went through the arches of hell, and methinks every harp in Heaven was silent, while a convulsive throb was felt in every angel's bosom, and a shadow of disappointment, wonder, and grief, passed over the features of the celestial host.

Eve soon appears in a new character With him her influence had ruined—she had gone forth an exile, with the curse of God. pursuing her—and became *a mother*. In some lonely valley, or on a mountain side of the world's vast wilderness, with no cheering accents but the voice of Adam, she brought forth her first-born. Never was there a more desolate mother. She had not even a manger, and the angels who fled affrighted when she sinned, came no more to cheer her solitude with their song of thanksgiving. She could pillow her aching head on the breast of Adam, but it brought only bitter recollections of brighter days. With maternal interest she might rejoice over the unconscious heir of frailty and suffering; but "*what will be his destiny* now we are fallen?" was a question that could not fail to oppress her loving heart. It would seem that Abel was a twin brother. Whether this were so or not, his name indicates that he was a weaker child and less tenderly loved. Eve centered her hopes in regard to the Redeemer and the honor of her family in Cain. How much this fact affected his character and cherished the haughty spirit which at length made him a fratricide, we cannot tell.

He may have apprehended something significant in the sacrifices, pointing to his own death as a type of the Great Sufferer. A dark thought had taken possession of his mind, and in sullen mood he set aside the authority of parental example in his offering to the Lord. Jehovah frowned upon him, while the smoke of his oblation ascended; but flooded with the smile of his approval the altar and the brow of Abel. In the conversation which followed, Cain became enraged, and smote his unoffending brother. When he saw the warm blood flowing from the wounds of his dying victim, and met the reproach of his fading eye, conscience with its terrors was let loose upon him, and branded by the wrath of God he fled a fugitive from the face of his kindred.

Adam in his customary walks, or led forth by the long absence of his sons into the fields, came suddenly upon the bloody corpse of Abel. He beheld the marks of violence, but the companion of the slain was gone; and while he knew that *death* had entered his family, it was *murder* too —the fearful harvest sown by parental transgression. It opened the ravages of crime, which were to make the green earth one wide field of battle. When the shock was over, and he recovered from his delirium of anguish, he bore the tidings to Eve.

Whether she was partially prepared for the bolt by his despairing face and incoherent expressions, or he rushed in the excess of his grief into her presence, with the shriek, "Abel *is dead!*" is left to conjecture. When the terrible fact *was* known, her heart sunk beneath the blow; for to the depth of a mother's sorrow was added the bitterness of *self-reproach.*

And that first funeral was a gloomy one —the uncoffined form was carried without a knell to its burial, and the shadow of a *grave* darkened a ruined world. Nor since has there been a sadder home or wilder lamentation, than that of the bereaved patriarch and his bewailing wife.

The years melted away, and Eve was again a mother. To her, evidently, was conceded the right of naming her offspring. This third son she called Seth, or *the appointed*, because God had given her another to fill the place of the departed. How beautifully this incident shows the maternal affection and trusting spirit of Eve! Her weary heart had a new object upon which to pour its wealth of love, and she recognized the hand of her injured Father in the bestowment of a blessing, which was to link her destiny with the advent of the promised Christ.

She lived to be the centre of a large domestic circle, and to behold the multiplying hundreds of a sinful and a suffering race. Bowed with the weight of years, and an experience full of the most varied and stirring events, she reached the limit of life. Oh! with what emotion she contemplated the past, while looking down into the gulf of dissolution. Around her lay the wreck of a planet which filled the universe with melody, when it rolled from the forming hand of God, and which in its moral destiny, had there been no interposition of grace, would have drifted forever from its orbit around His Throne. Her children and friends gathered about her dying couch, to hear her last accents and receive her blessing. Adam, leaning upon his staff, stood by her pillow and bedewed her pale forehead with his tears, breathing in her ear comforting words concerning the mercy of the Lord.

In the struggles of that hour, Eve could lean alone upon the promise of a Messiah to come—the only ray penetrating the dark valley was that dim revelation of a Saviour who would be the "resurrection and the life." She cast a mournful glance upon those she had loved and ruined, murmured a farewell, looked upward with a smile of victory, and the conflict was over—*the mother of mankind was no more.*

The tidings spread, and from the scattered dwellings of her descendants was heard the voice of weeping—for Eve had been loved for her affectionate fidelity to Adam, and her tender solicitude for the happiness of all. Beside she retained traces of her primeval beauty, and subdued by penitence, she lived among them a model of matronly dignity, meekness and piety. Her solemn counsels and many prayers were remembered, and her frailty in the ruinous experiment of disobedience, was well nigh forgotten in the grief of an *orphan race.* In silence, except the sobs of unaffected mourning, she was borne to her grave beside that of the martyred Abel.

Though no epitaph was written, as often as the eye of the passer-by fell upon that mound, or the foliage waving over it, he read the language of those words written in burning capitals over the gateway of despair—"In the day that thou eatest thereof, THOU SHALT SURELY DIE."

SARAI was a Hebrew maiden of remarkable beauty. Her childhood and youth were passed among the mountains of Armenia, whose fine climate and sublime scenery developed her form and gave strength to her intellectual powers. Her noble figure, dark eye luminous with expression, and the graceful dignity of her manner, made her the admiration of the Chaldean shepherds and the pride of her kindred.

Among the wealthy nomads of the fruitful valleys who sought her hand in marriage, was Abram, a kinsman. A worshipper of the infinite One, he loved her for her elevated piety, no less than for her personal beauty. And doubtless they often walked forth together beneath the nightly sky, whose transparent air in that latitude made the stars impressively—

"The burning blazonry of God!"

Upon the hill-tops around, were the observatories and altars of Chaldean philosophy, whose disciples worshipped the host of Heaven. In the serenity of such an hour, with the white tents reposing in the distance, and the "soul-like sound" of the rustling forest alone breaking the stillness, it would not be strange as they gazed on flaming Orion and the Pleiades if *they* had bowed with the devotee of Light, while

> "Beneath his blue and beaming sky,
> He worshipped at their lofty shrine,
> And deemed he saw with gifted eye,
> The Godhead in his works divine."

But a purer illumination than streamed from that radiant dome, brought near in his ineffable majesty the Eternal, and like the holy worshippers of Eden, they adored with subdued and reverent hearts, their infinite Father.

To a reflective mind, there is great sublimity and impressiveness in the purity and growth of religious principle, in circumstances so adverse to its manifestation. The temptations resisted—the earnest communion with each other—the glorious aspirations and soarings of imagination, when morning broke upon the girdling summits, and when evening came down with its stars, and its rising moon, flooding with glory nature in her repose; these and a thousand lovely and touching scenes of that pastoral life are all unrecorded. The great events in history, and bold points in character, are seized by the inspired penman as sufficient to sweep the grand outline of God's providential and moral government over the world, and his care of his people.

Just when it would best accomplish his designs, which are ever marching like destiny to their fulfilment, Jehovah called to Abram, and bade him go to a distant land which he would show him. With his father-in-law and with Lot, his flocks and herds, he journeyed toward Palestine.— When he arrived at Haran, in Mesopotamia, pleased with the country, and probably influenced by the declining health of the aged Terah, he took up his residence there. Here he remained till the venerable patriarch, Sarai's father, died. The circle of relatives bore him to the grave, and kept the days of mourning. But the dutiful daughter wept in the solitary grief of an orphan's heart. A few years before, she had lost a brother, and now the father to whom she was the last flower that bloomed on the desert of age, and who lavished his love upon her, was buried among strangers.

Then the command to move forward to his promised inheritance came again to Abram. Sarai shed upon that lonely grave the baptism of her tears, and turned away in the sad beauty of mourning to fold her tent and enter the shadows of an untravelled wilderness. They journeyed on among the hills, encamping at night beside a mountain spring, and beneath the unclouded heavens arching their path, changeless and watchful as the love of God—exiles by the power of their simple faith in him. Soon as they reached Palestine, Abram consecrated its very soil by erecting a family altar, first in the plain of Moreh, and again on the summits that catch the smile of morning near the hamlet of Bethel.

Months stepped away rapidly as silently, old associations wore off, and Abram was a wealthy and happy man in the luxuriant vales of Canaan. His flocks dotted the plains, and his cattle sent down their lowing from encircling hills. But more than these to him was the affection of his beautiful wife. Her eye watched his form along the winding way, when with the ascending sun he went out on the dewy slopes; and kindled with a serene welcome when at night-fall he returned for repose amid the sacred joys of home.

At length there came on a fearful famine. The rain was withholden, and the dew shed its benediction no more upon the earth. He was compelled to seek bread at the court of Pharaoh, or perish. Knowing the power of female beauty, and the want of principle among the Egyptian princes, he feared assassination and the captivity of Sarai which would follow. Haunted with this apprehension, he told her to affirm upon inquiry that she was his sister—which was not a direct falsehood, but only so by *implication*. According to the Jewish mode of reckoning she might be called a sister, and Abram stooped to this prevarication under that terrible excitement of fear, which, in the case of Peter, drove a true disciple of Christ to the brink of apostasy and despair.

But his deception involved him in the very difficulty he designed to escape. The king's courtiers saw the handsome Hebrew, and extolled her beauty before him. He summoned her to the apartments of the palace, and captivated by her loveliness, determined to make her his bride. During the agonizing suspense of Abram, and the concealed anguish of Sarai in her conscious degradation, the hours wore heavily away, until the judgments of God upon the royal household brought deliverance. Pharaoh, though an idolater, knew by this supernatural infliction, that there was guilt in the transaction, and called Abram to an account. He had nothing to say in self-acquittal, and with a strange magnanimity, was sent away with his wife and his property quietly; followed only by the reproaches of Pharaoh, and his own wakeful conscience.

Abram returned to Palestine, became a victor in fierce battles with a vastly outnumbering foe, and was in possession of a splendid fortune. Yet Sarai was unhappy because she was childless. She had the Lord's promise that a son should beguile the hours of declining life, but the years fled, and there was no token of fulfilment.

In her disappointment and impatience she told her husband it was folly to hope on, and pointed to Hagar, a servant, as the mother of the expected heir. By following his suggestion in Egypt she went to the verge of ruin, and now in turn is the tempter, involving her family in guilt and discord that almost broke the heart of Abram. When the slave was likely to bear a son, her vanity was excited, and she treated Sarai with scorn that roused her indignation. Hagar was banished and became a friendless fugitive in the wilderness—where the angel of God found her weary and fainting, led her to a gushing spring, and there bade her go back submissively to her mistress.

Soon after Jehovah appeared to Abram in a glorious vision, talking with him as friend to friend. He fell on his face in the dust, as did the exile of Patmos ages after, while a voice of affection and hope, came from the bending sky—"I am the Almighty God; walk before me and be thou perfect." The solemn covenant involving the greatness and splendor of the people and commonwealth that should spring from the solitary pair, was renewed; and as an outward seal, he was named Abraham, *The father of a great multitude*—and his wife Sarah, *The princess*. Still he laughed at the absurdity that Sarah would ever be a mother, and invoked a blessing on Ishmael, but evidently said nothing to her upon a subject dismissed as incredible from his thoughts. For when the celestial messengers were in the tent on their way to warn Lot, she listened to their earnest conversation, concealed by the curtains, and hearing that repeated promise based on the immutability of God, also laughed with bitter mirth, at her hopeless prospect in regard to the marvellous prediction. And when one of the Angels, who was Jehovah veiled in human form, as afterwards "manifest in the flesh," charged her with this unbelief and levity, the discovery roused her fears, and approaching him, without hesitation, she denied the fact. He knew perfectly her sudden apprehension, and only repeated the accusation, enforced doubtless by a glance of omniscience, like that which pierced the heart of Peter.

The group separated, and two of those bright beings went on to Sodom. The next morning Abraham walked out upon the plain, and looked towards the home of Lot. He saw the smoke as of a great furnace going up to the calm azure, from the scathed and blackened plains where life was so busy and joyous a few hours before! With a heavy heart he returned to his tent, and brought Sarah forth to behold the scene. She clung with trembling to his side, while she listened to the narration of the terrible overthrow of those gorgeous cities, and the rescue of her brother's household, and beheld in the distance the seething and silent grave of millions, sending up a swaying column of ebon, cloud-like incense to God's burning indignation against sin.

They left the vale of Mamre, and journeyed to Gera, where, with a marvellous forgetfulness of the past, the beauty of Sarah again led them into deception and falsehood, and with the same result as before. Abimelech, the king, would have taken her for his wife as Abraham's sister, had not God appeared in a dream threatening immediate death. Upon pleading his innocence he was spared, and expostulating with his guest, generously offered him a choice of residence in the land; but rebuked Sarah with merited severity.

Prophecy and covenant now hastened to

their fulfilment. Sarah gave birth to a son, and with the name of God on her lips, she gave utterance to holy rapture. With all her faults, she was a pious and noble woman. She meant to train him for the Lord, and therefore when she saw young Ishmael mocking at the festival of his weaning, she besought her husband to send away the irreverent son, whose influence might ruin the consecrated Isaac. Hagar, with a generous provision for her wants, was once more a fugitive; and the Most High approved the solicitude of a mother for an only child, around whose destiny was gathered the interest of ages, and the hopes of a world.

And now, with the solemn shadows of life's evening hours falling around her, and a heart subdued by the discipline of Providence, in the fullness of love which had been rising so long within the barriers of hope deferred, she bent prayerfully over the very slumbers of that fair boy, and taught him the precious name of God, with the first prattle of his infant lips. How proudly she watched the unfolding of this bud of promise. When in the pastimes of childhood, he played before the tent-door, or with a shout of gladness ran to meet Abraham returning from the folds, her calm and glowing eye marked his footsteps, and her grateful aspirations for a blessing on the lad went up to the Heaven of heavens. At length he stood before her in the manliness and beauty of youth unscarred by the rage of passions, and with a brow open and laughing as the radiant sky of his own lovely Palestine.

It was a morning which flooded the dewy plains with glory, and filled the groves with music, when Abraham came in from his wonted communion with God, and called for Isaac, and told him to prepare for a three days' journey into the wilderness. How tenderly was Sarah regarded in this scene of trial. Evidently no information of the awful command to sacrifice the son of her old age, was made to her. She might have read something fearful in the lines of anxious thought and the workings of deep emotion in the face of Abraham. But he evaded all inquiries on the subject, "clave the wood," and accompanied by two of his young men, turned from his dwelling with a blessing from that wondering mother, and was soon lost from her straining vision among the distant hills. Upon the third day he saw the top of Mount Moriah kindling in the rising sun, and taking Isaac alone, ascended to the summit, whereon was to be reared an altar, which awakened more intense solicitude in heaven, than any offering before or since, except on Calvary, where God's "only-begotten and well-beloved son" was slain. There is no higher moral sublimity, than the unwavering trust and cheerful obedience of this patriarch, when the very oath of the Almighty seemed perjured, and the bow of promise blotted from the firmament of faith! But he believed Jehovah, and would have clung to his assurance, though the earth had reeled in her orbit, and every star drifted from its moorings. He prayed for strength, with his hand on the forehead of his submissive son.

> " He rose up and laid
> The wood upon the altar. All was done,
> He stood a moment—and a deep, quick flush
> Passed o'er his countenance; and then he nerved
> His spirit with a bitter strength, and spoke—
> " Isaac! my only son"—The boy looked up,
> And Abraham turned his face away and wept.
> " Where is the lamb, my father?"—O, the tones,
> The sweet, the thrilling music of a child!
> How it doth agonize at such an hour!
> It was the last, deep struggle—Abraham held
> His loved, his beautiful, his only son,

And lifted up his arm, and called on God—
And lo! God's Angel staid him—and he fell
Upon his face and wept."

When on his return he told Sarah of his strange mission, and how the Lord stayed his uplifted hand when the struggle had passed, with deeper yearnings of the maternal heart she clasped Isaac to her bosom, and mingled with his own, her tears of joy. She did not long survive this last test of fidelity, itself the crowning evidence that she was the mother whose posterity would out-number the stars. At Kirjath-arba, in the vale of Hebron, during the absence of Abraham, Sarah died. When he heard of her death, he hastened to her burial, "to mourn and to weep for her." There is no more affecting funeral scene in history. Bending over the corpse of his beautiful and devoted wife, he looked upon the strangers about him, and while his hoary locks shook with the excitement of grief, he sobbed aloud, "I am a stranger and a sojourner with you; give me a possession of a burying place with you, that I may bury my dead out of my sight."

He bought the field of Machpelah, and in a cave, which seemed to have been formed for a sepulchre, beneath the shade of forest trees, he laid the form he loved when a beauteous maiden, the noblest of wives, and a faithful, praying mother. With Isaac weeping at his side, he turned away to enforce on his tender spirit her holy counsels, and wait further upon the providence of God toward the youth; upon whom must fall the patriarchal mantle, and who was to guard and transmit the knowledge and worship of Jehovah.

It was sunset on the plains of Mesopotamia. Around them stood the mountains, with their brows bathed in the glow of an oriental day, as it dropped gloriously behind them. Far down their darkening sides, the flocks were gathering to their folds, and with a softened murmur the echoes went up from the distant city in the vale of Haran, towards whose gates from the interlocking hills of the south, wound slowly a strange cavalcade. The camels were laden richly, and walked wearily, for they had travelled from Palestine, which was more than four hundred miles from Haran. They were led by an aged man of patriarchal air, whose calm face revealed both a thoughtful mind, and the dignity of goodness; while his flowing beard fell upon his breast white as a wreath of snow. He was the faithful steward of Abraham, and with an oath of fidelity in his mission, journeyed to the land of Nahor to choose a bride for Isaac, worthy of the honor, and educated in the religion of his father. The shadows of twilight were deepening upon the landscape, when he passed beside a well in the suburbs of the city, and gazed upon its walls with the intense emotion which agitates the heart, when the conflict between hope and fear is drawing to a final issue. And besides his contemplations of the Invisible, he had but one thought during all his days of lonely travel, and his nights of wakefulness beneath the beaming sky above his roofless head: "Where shall I find the maiden my master will approve, and his only son receive to his home, as the *second princess* in their illustrious line? It was the time of evening when the women came out to draw water, and he determined to make the occasion decisive, under the direction of God.

He made the camels kneel about him, and bowing himself in prayer, he besought the Lord "to give him speed" in the matter for Abraham, his servant's sake. It was no formal prayer he breathed upon the quiet air, which scarcely lifted the hoary locks from his anxious brow. It was no wavering faith that cast all the care of his troubled spirit on Jehovah, desiring the sign of his approval in a simple expression of Eastern hospitality. And while he was communing with God, Rebekah the daughter of Bethuel, came out bearing her pitcher; and, "the damsel was *very fair to look upon.*" Her singular beauty arrested the eye of Eliezer. He watched her while she ran to the fountain, so airily,

> "The light spring-flower would scarcely bow
> Beneath her step,"—

and stooped to the waters, like a white swan bending to the glassy wave. Then lifting the pitcher to her shoulder, upon which the raven ringlets fell wavingly from her fair forehead, she stood before him in the fading light, the impersonation of virgin loveliness. She did not see the charmed Eliezer, and hastened nymph-like along her star-lit path, towards the city gate. Starting as from a dream, he ran forward to meet her, and asked permission to drink of the water. She immediately dropped the pitcher upon her hand and said, "Drink, my lord." Just then she observed the panting camels, and with the same disinterested kindness, and a voice which was the very music of love, offered to draw water "for them also, until they had done drinking." He was so absorbed by a solemn interest of which she knew nothing, that "he held his peace," without even rendering aid to Rebekah; but mutely admiring her faultless person, and generous deed, he wondered if that beautiful being *was* the object of his toilsome pilgrimage. She had given the sign unconsciously, of his own choosing, and the fact gradually spread hopeful tranquillity over his bewildered thought. He gave her an ear-ring of pure gold, and a pair of costly bracelets, inquiring after her father's house, and if he could have entertainment there for the night. The maiden modestly told her lineage, assuring him both of a kind reception and abundant provision for his animals. When he knew it was the family of Nahor, the pious and shrewd old man doubted no more, but recognized the hand of the Lord. He bowed in grateful adoration on the dewy earth, amid the stillness of nature reposing upon the bosom of God, and poured forth from a full heart his thanksgiving. Rebekah ran to her mother, told her what had happened, and the mysterious words the man had spoken. This simple incident is a sweet glimpse at the amiable and filial character of Milcah's daughter.

While they were talking over the marvellous occurrence, Laban, a brother, went out to see who the wealthy stranger might be, and learn his design in visiting their beautiful city. Doubtless he was more interested in the shekels of gold than the *devotional* expressions his sister repeated.

But when he found him at the well, in the apparent disinterestedness of a true patriarch, with a benediction, he bade him come to his dwelling, for every preparation was made for his accommodation. Soon the girdle and sandals were removed, and he was invited to partake of the evening repast. And now appears the *tact*, eloquence, and religious principle of this servant, which were evidently the ground of Abraham's confidence in his management, in the discourse and special pleading before the household of his entertainer.

With solemnity becoming his responsibility, he refused to eat till he had made known his errand. He then introduces himself as the servant of Abraham, who by the blessing of God, he adds, "is become great." After describing the magnitude of his vast possessions, he makes a graceful transition to Isaac, the sole heir of this fame and splendid inheritance. He gives the reason for his long journey in search of a bride, the irreligious character of the Canaanites, narrating the conversation with his master, and the hesitation he felt in entering upon the delicate undertaking. The entire scene at the well is minutely delineated, to convince them that the Almighty had sanctioned the transaction, and bestowed unequivocal signs of his approbation of the choice. Without doubt, he marked the impression his address made on the listening group, and was not afraid to throw the entire matter upon their decision. He had completely won the father and brother to his purpose, and they referred the whole question to Rebekah. There was a struggle in the mother's bosom, and Rebekah hung upon her neck in tears. Eliezer evidently regarded the matter as settled, and distributed with princely liberality his magnificent presents among the members of the family.

At a late hour they retired for repose, but how little slumber in that dwelling! The successful servant may have fallen into pleasant dreams, Bethuel and Laban, proud of the prospective alliance, may have slept, thronged with golden visions; but the heart of the maiden never beat so wildly before, and life assumed a strange reality, to her musing and restless spirit. The mother was sorrowful and prayerful, for an only daughter was the sacrifice demanded, and sending her to Canaan, was like burying her from sight forever.

In the morning came the final trial—when God's eternal puposes were borne onward by the unostentatious incidents of a touching domestic scene. And who can tell the influence, though unseen, of the history of any family upon the destinies of a succeeding generation! Eliezer signified the necessity of his immediate departure. Milcah and Laban besought him to tarry a few days, for they could not part thus suddenly with the damsel. But there were mightier interests than those of time at stake, and he was firm in his purpose. Rebekah was called, and asked if she were willing to go immediately with the man. She was prepared by a higher communion than that with kindred, and the heroism of cheerful piety, to answer unhesitatingly, "*I will go.*" When the circumstances are considered, there is here a moral sublimity, pure and impressive, as that which hung around the first female who abandoned the land of her birth and the friendships of home, for the wide ocean, and a grave on plains overshadowed by the temples of idol-worship.

With blessings upon her head, and tearful adieus, in her queenly womanhood, the more beautiful for her sadness, she mounted the kneeling camel, and accompanied by the nurse of her infancy, and the retinue that came to escort her, moved silently from the city of her fathers. And how often with swimming eye, she turned to gaze on the receding valley, upon whose peaceful breast, like a white speck, lay the beloved city. But a new world soon spread around the fair traveller. Sometimes wild summits cast their shadows upon her way; then from a hill-top she looked off upon luxuriant plains, with their isles of foliage dallying with the passing wind, and a horizon of mountains pencilled on the haze of the dreamy sky. And there were hours when her thoughts wandered from all these, and brooded with painful intensity upon her unfolding destiny.

It was eventide of such a day as dawns on Palestine, when Rebekah saw in the distance, a man in meditative mood, walking in the fields. With that presentiment which seemed often almost prophetic when near an expected event, and probably aided by the indication of devotional spirit, she suspected him to be Isaac, and alighted from her camel. Eliezer confirmed her suspicions, and veiling herself, she modestly awaited his approach. He was a stranger, and might not fall in with her guide's admiration—or there might be something in him repulsive to her own taste.

While these conflicting emotions were passing, Eliezer had informed Isaac of his travels, the interview with Rebekah at the well, the objections he overruled in obtaining consent of her relatives, and the sad farewells that still haunted his memory. Isaac felt that the Almighty, whose voice he heard when on the altar of Moriah, had brought him a wife, he could love for her own sake, and he took her joyfully to his tent. It was the very place where Sarah died, and he had mourned deeply for his sainted mother. Rebekah came to his solitude, like an angel of consolation, and his pensive home was lighted with a smile of returning hope. Time passed on, and with all his riches, there were hours of sadness in that home, because no children were given him. He prayed earnestly for the covenant blessing, and Rebekah bore him twins, who were named Esau and Jacob—the beginning of sorrows to her, and of suffering to them all, till they slept in death. The sons grew to manhood—Esau, the inheritor of the birthright, was a sportsman, and a passionate man, but the favorite of Isaac because he gratified his father's fondness for venison; Jacob, a quiet shepherd, became the idol of his mother;—a parental partiality, which resulted at length in the overthrow of Esau, while his brother rose upon his ruin.

Driven by famine like Abraham before him, to seek bread at a foreign court, the patriarch went to Gerar. Apprehensive of assassination on account of Rebekah's beauty, he also was guilty of the cowardly act of dissembling, in which she was accessory. She told the admiring princes that Isaac was a brother. Abimelech the king discovered the deception accidentally, and bitterly reproved the stranger. It is somewhat remarkable, that the grand trio of primal patriarchs, married handsome women; who, notwithstanding their exalted character and fidelity, cost two of them days of gloomy fear, and crime that left ever after burning on the conscience, the living coals of remorse.

Isaac now reached his dotage; feeble and blind, he knew death was near. He called

Esau, and told him as he might die suddenly, to get him venison and prepare for the solemn occasion of receiving his parting blessing, which should secure the privileges and pre-eminence of the first-born. The hunter went into the fields; and Rebekah, recollecting that Jacob had purchased the birthright of his brother for a mess of pottage, one day when he came in from the chase faint with hunger and exhaustion, determined by a stroke of management to seal with the patriarchal benediction, that transfer of the unappreciated distinction by Esau, who was disinclined manifestly, to a religious life.

She sent him to the flocks after two kids, which were prepared with the savory delicacy his father loved, and assuming the responsibility of any anathema that might follow, she dressed him up in Esau's apparel, covering his hands and neck to imitate the hairiness of the rightful heir, and sent him to the bedside of the dying Isaac. When the patriarch inquired who he was, he replied, "I am Esau, thy first-born." This was passing belief, because even the skilful hunter, could scarcely without a miracle so soon bring in the game, and dress it for his table. Jacob was called to his side, and he felt of his hands; the disguise completed the delusion, although his voice had the milder tone of the young shepherd, to that father's ear. He repeated the interrogation concerning his name, then embracing him, pronounced in a strain of true poetry, the perpetual blessing of Jehovah's favor upon his undertakings, and his posterity. The stratagem had succeeded, and Jacob hastened to inform his mother of the victory, just as Esau returned. When Isaac discovered the mistake, he trembled with excitement, while his son cried in anguish, "Bless even me also, O my father!" That cry pierced the breaking heart of the aged man, but it was a fruitless lament. He was inflexible, and Esau wept aloud over his blasted hopes; plotting at the same time, in his awakened enmity, the murder of Jacob. Rebekah was alarmed at his fury, and sent "the supplanter," to her kindred in Haran of Mesopotamia.

Her tent was now a spot of deepening gloom; there were hours of mournful meditation in the apartment of approaching dissolution, and of weeping in the solitude of the noble yet erring mother. Though strangely fallen from her youthful purity, she exhibited decided religious principle in her grief, when Esau to obtain revenge for her neglect of his boyhood, married an idolater. Accumulating troubles, made her weary of life, but where or when she died, the sacred historian has not given the slightest intimation. There is something significant in the fact, which justifies the inference, that her departure was a dreary one—cheered only by penitential trust in the Lord. It may be that she was glad to leave a pathway on which the morning of her existence shed a heavenly radiance, but which, strewed with the sere leaves of blighted innocence and hope, met the grave o'erclouded with sorrow, and wet with tears.

As a maiden, Rebekah was a model, an acknowledged beauty, and amiable in all the relations of life. She was a devoted wife, and only when corrupted by favoritism towards Jacob, and the example of Isaac in falsehood, did her character as a mother pass under eclipse. The crowning act of her guilty fondness and ambition, was *presumption*. Because God had made known his purpose to reverse the rule of primogeniture in her family, she determined in her own way to carry out the design. This one object took possession of her mind, until like a kind of madness, it urged her onward to crimes that made existence a burden, and which invested with a painful uncertainty her abode in the world to come.

A CENTURY after the matrimonial embassy from Palestine halted at nightfall before the city of Nahor, a solitary fugitive soon after noon of a sultry day, dusty and worn with travel, joined a group of shepherds, who waited with their flocks beside a well in the same valley of Haran. He fled from an angry brother, and had wandered for weeks among the hills, cheered at night while reposing on the ground, with the glories of Heaven whose gates were thrown wide open above him. The angels upon a stair-way of light, came in throngs from the celestial plains, fanning his throbbing brow with their wings, and chasing from his spirit sad thoughts with the ravishing melody of their sinless abode. On a throne such as was never piled for human sovereignty, he beheld the Almighty enrobed with splendors that put out the stars, and heard the accents of sympathy and promise from his lips.

Thus sustained in his banishment, and bound by an oath made at the bedside of his dying father, to marry among his kindred of Mesopotamia, Jacob rested, a friendless exile, by the fountain where the camels of the servant Eliezer knelt laden with precious gifts. It was a strange contrast in life, especially when equal honor was the inheritance. The lesson taught then, as now, was the unerring providence of God amid the mutations of time, and the folly of desponding when a cloud blackens on the horizon of the future.

The traveller inquired after the health of Laban. The Chaldeans answered his inquiries, and pointing to a beautiful shepherdess coming with her flock, told him there was Rachel his daughter. With that courtesy which springs from magnanimity of spirit and needs only the culture of opportunity to develop itself, Jacob hastened to the well, rolled away the stone, and watered her sheep. The intelligence he had received, stirred the depths of his spirit, as the storm moves the sea, for in all his wanderings he met with no familiar face, nor heard one accent of affection. Saluting his fair cousin with a kiss, he lifted up his voice and wept. The recollections of home, the present joyful surprise, and visions of the future, swept like a rushing tide over his sad heart. When the agitation subsided and he could command utterance, he disclosed his relationship, by tenderly alluding to his mother, Laban's only sister, with whom he parted while the bloom of girlhood was yet upon her cheek. Breathless with excitement and delight, she flew to her father with the tidings. He welcomed the young man to his dwelling, and invited him to become a resident in Haran, offering as an inducement to pay him his own price for labor.

Jacob was smitten with Rachel's beauty, and the sweetness of her temper, and immediately consented on condition that he might marry her as the reward of seven years, toil. The days went by on rainbow wing, and the time of service vanished like a dream. When he came in at evening, her beaming eye was upon him—and often till " the noon of night" the hours were passed in companionship unsullied by suspicion, while they talked of their love, the strange vicissitudes of their kindred, and the bright displays of Jehovah's regard. Jacob was a true-hearted and godly man. He once yielded to temptation presented by *a mother*, and was guilty of duplicity that cost him his self-respect, and made him despise her; but ever after exhibited a lofty integrity both as a citizen and a devout patriarch.

At length he claimed his bride. The marriage festival was magnificent, and the exile of Canaan the central object of its gay assemblage. The evening waned, the lamps burned dimly, and music died away as with very weariness, when the parting salutations were exchanged around the wedded twain. But by an act of basest deception, Laban compelled Jacob to take Leah, an older daughter, for his wife, because customary to give the eldest first in marriage. So strong was his affection for Rachel, he suppressed his indignation and engaged to work another seven years for her. In condemning this unnatural polygamy, two things are to be considered; the fraud of the father in withholding the first choice, and the absence of any established principles of civil or religious polity. There is a tendency in the mind to bring those ancient worthies for judgment, from the twilight of their dispensation to the foot of Sinai, and even to the Cross of Messiah, where we sit in the blaze of the gospel's noontide, and learn the precepts of immaculate widom.

Rachel, though evidently less amiable than Leah, reigned in the affections of Jacob. When her envy and impatience because her sister bare sons and she was childless, found expression in reproach of her husband, and a wish to die if longer unblest, his anger called forth but a mild rebuke.

Twenty years passed by, and Jacob, a wealthy patriarch, departed from Haran as he came, a fugitive from kindred. And as before in his flight, nightly repose brought visions of paradise, and the voice of God. He was overtaken by his pursuers, and accused among other things of stealing Laban's teraphim. From some unknown motive, Rachel had carried away these household gods, and dissembled, to conceal the fact. But the blemishes on her character, when the attention and flattery her beauty received are taken into the account, are faint and few. She was a splendid woman, beloved in all the relations of domestic and social life.

At the ford of Jabbok, when Jacob was about to encounter the embittered Esau with his host, he placed in the rear of his own caravan, Rachel and the stripling Joseph, her youngest boy, to have them the least exposed if an attack were made.— How remote the thought, when she led the lad to the margin of the stream, that his infant hand would in after years, hold the key of a monarch's treasury, wanting only a sceptre to be Sovereign of the proudest realm on earth, rescuing from famine Israel and his household, to prevent the failure of a single promise concerning the chosen of the Lord.

Not far from Bethel, Rachel gave birth to another son—and her own life was the price of this last-born. Having escaped the rage of enemies, and the perils of a wearisome march, just entering into the very bosom of Canaan, Rachel must be laid in the grave. She was conscious of her hastening dissolution, and murmured *Benoni—the son of my sorrow.* Then with a blessing, she bade

Jacob and her noble sons farewell, looked up trustingly to the sky bending brightly above her, and "fell asleep." Her last gaze was towards the hills around Bethlehem, which were flooded with the light of the star in the East, and echoed back to the "Mount of God" the chorus of angels, when "He who should redeem Israel" was cradled in a manger! They buried her there, and Jacob erected a memorial of stone, which survived the lapse of centuries, and was cherished as the monument of beauty and worth by his descendants, till it crumbled to dust.

We need no further illustration of her elevated character than those testimonials, or of her intellectual force and piety than the faultless and kingly Joseph—the full-length portrait of a pure and brilliant man, which in the distance and dimness of antiquity, is yet distinct and beautiful, beneath the radiance that falls from the Eternal city of the better Canaan, into which he entered.

DESTINY, in the history of an individual and a nation, often turns on apparently an unimportant event. We have in Revelation impressive illustrations of this truth; as if God, by poising his own stupendous plans on the common occurrences of life, would teach man his particular providence, and the solemnity of action on the stage of probation, where the very echo of his footsteps will be heard forever.

The fulfilment of prophecy, and the greatness and glory of the Hebrew nation, were all involved in the preservation of a single man-child among thousands with whom it was doomed to a violent death. For three months parental love had eluded the edict of the tyrant who "knew not Joseph," till concealment was no longer an experiment of hope. The beautiful child was enclosed in a bark of rushes, and committed to the bosom of the Nile. Miriam, an only sister, was sent to watch the frail vessel, while it floated down the lazy current, the plaything of every ripple,

"And every breath of air that chanced to blow."

It was to avoid suspicion that Jochebed remained at home, to indulge a mother's grief, and lift to Israel's God a mother's prayer. And Miriam, a summer day rambler among the flags by the river's margin, or fragrant wild flowers beneath the branching palm, would not arrest the eye of the passing Egyptian. How strangely the bloom of girlhood upon her cheek contrasted with the tear-drops trembling on the long lashes, which almost veiled the glance following ever the boat of that young dreamer. An oriental sky bends brightly above her, and the waters sparkle as if in very gladness, around the boy—

> "The whispering reeds are all *he* hears,
> The Nile's soft weltering nigh
> Sings him to sleep;"—

but *her* heart beats audibly, and dark thoughts of man and of life are chasing away a thousand glowing visions of the future.

The day wore on, the sun bathed his burning forehead in the Mediterranean sea, and threw the glory of his farewell upon the hills that border on the fruitful valley, whose soil was wet with the blood of her countrymen. She heard the murmur of voices, and the sound of coming footsteps startling her from a mournful reverie. Pale with fear, she stood like the hunted fawn in his glade, panting before his pursuers. The little Levite, perhaps, was slumbering his last, and would be an evening sacrifice at the hand of the hastening executioner.

When she saw the form of the king's daughter followed by her maidens, hope stilled her fluttering heart. The princess *might* take her bath without observing the barge of bulrushes—if she did make the discovery, woman's heart was moved by an infant's smile, and touched by its cry.

The tiny ark *was* seen, and brought to the bank. The babe opened his blue eye on the wondering women and wept, for among them all no maternal arms were extended in welcome, nor familiar voice fell on the ear of the Hebrew's son.

But he had won the royal sympathy; Miriam knew he was safe, and asked permission to find a nurse. With joy that spoke in every lineament of her face, and the fleetness of her arrow-like step, she returned to the dwelling she left in sorrow, and Jochebed soon clasped the child to her heaving breast, naming him Moses—*drawn from the water*. Pharaoh's daughter bade her train him for her father's palace, and bring him there when he reached his boyhood.

Miriam rose to womanhood with a tone of masculine beauty, and Moses, a manly youth, took an honorable position in the court of Pharaoh. The influences of home were inwrought with all his sympathies, and he looked with deepest scorn upon a despot's favor and a splendid career, while the groans of his oppressed people were filling the heavens. Possessing the traits of a hero in the highest degree, Jehovah by a visible manifestation appointed him chieftain, to strike for the deliverance of his nation.

He stood with Aaron before the haughty monarch, cheered doubtless by the remembered words of Miriam who had felt the bitterness of oppression, and a mother's blessing, and boldly announced the command of God to let Israel go. Pharaoh poured contempt on the message and Him who sent it. Moses lifted up his rod, and the Nile on which he floated in helpless infancy, with every streamlet and pool, was turned into blood! But the king was unmoved when his fears were gone. Fire and hail descended in a tempest, and ran in torrents upon the blackening plains. Darkness deeper than broods on mornless chaos blotted out the stars, and quenched the flame of his brightest lamps—but not until the first-born of every Egyptian household in his realm lay a stiffened corpse, as a fearful atonement for the innocents he had slain, did he consent to the departure of his God-protected slaves.

They reached the sea, which spread its waste of billows between them and Canaan. Again the mysterious rod was raised over the waters, and they rolled up like mighty scrolls on each hand, and stood in walls of crystal beside their paved and ample path. The grand procession, with flying banners and silent march, wound like a vast Hydra through that parted deep. Just as Moses went up the opposing bank, Pharaoh's pursuing host, with exultant shouts and the noise of numberless chariot wheels, poured into the gorge of uplifted waves. He stretched out the rod once more towards his foes, and with the crash of a thousand besieged and falling towers, the billowy mountains fell on that rushing army. Banner and plume—the horse and his rider—weapons of war and shivered chariots, were mingled in a common wreck, and the requiem was the shrieks and curses of dying men, and the roar of foam-wreathed surges. The trembling multitudes of Israel from their peaceful shore looked mutely on, till that mournful cadence rose faintly on the troubled air.

"Then sang Moses and the children of Israel unto the Lord" an anthem of unequalled sublimity—and Miriam, inspired with prophetic fire, "took a timbrel in her hand; and all the women went out after her, with timbrels and with dances." She threw in a chorus worthy the theme and the occasion; the wilderness sent up echoes which never before stirred its solitude, and the notes of rapture floated in a tide of melody over the solemn sea, which was now the grave of an imperial army. That song and response were composed six hundred years before the immortal Grecian swept his wondrous harp in his blindness, and yet in grandeur that towers to the Throne of God, and power that thrills like a trumpet-blast, it leaves the wandering bard in the low grounds of mortal conflict, or on the sunny mount of contending gods.

It is sad to turn from that jubilant procession led on by the fair prophetess, to the scene of her fall. The Israelites reached the wilderness of Zin, and encamped on its extended plain. On each side stood the sentinel mountains, whose helmets of rock rent the folds of the summer cloud as it passed; the standards were unfurled, and the Tabernacle set up. Miriam had seen Moses robed in lightning on the smoking top of Sinai, and listened to the message from his lips when his brow shone like an angel's—she had loved him as a part of her own being since her lonely vigil by the river's side—but now ambition stalked through the chambers of her soul like a sceptered king, made the affections its vassals, and was environed by the train of riotous passions. Under the new arrangement adopted by Moses at the suggestion of Jethro, his father-in-law, the power was divided among captains, and her authority weakened. Besides, she had marked with jealousy the presence of Zipporah the Ethiopian in the camp, receiving the attention of the great leader, and the admiration of the multitude.

She went to Aaron, and "spoke against Moses." He listened to the complaint, which was an appeal to his own wounded honor, and a conspiracy was matured. The Lawgiver was meek in his majesty, and unsullied by human praise or earthly distinction. He met the frown of the conspirators with unshadowed benignity, nor did their reproaches disturb the tranquillity of his spirit. One morning, a voice from the opening heavens commanded Moses, Aaron and Miriam, to go up to the tabernacle of the congregation. Then amid strange spreadings of light, a cloud descended and hung over that sanctuary of the Shekinah which was glowing with purple and blue and embroidered with gold. Silence hung upon the vast assembly, while the three passed in wondering stillness to the open court. Pausing there, Moses stood in the calmness of innocence, his noble figure enveloped in a simple mantle. Aaron was arrayed in his sacerdotal robes flashing with jewels and fringed with golden bells. Between them was the ambitious Miriam, richly apparelled, and sullen in her pride and awakened fears.

That radiant column of cloud filled the door of the tabernacle, and the Almighty spoke from its form reflecting the glory that mantles His Throne. He called Aaron and Miriam into its mysterious folds, and alluding to the evidences of the celestial commission of their brother, and assuring them that with none other did he talk as friend with friend, inquired if they were not afraid to reproach his servant.

Whether with a thunder peal or a blaze of Omniscience he displayed his anger, we know not. But he manifested his kindled indignation, and departed. The cloud rose and vanished from the sight of the gazing tribes, and Miriam was a leper, "white as snow." Aaron beheld her, and fell at the feet of Moses, beseeching him to intercede with God. Miriam was mute, for she was a fallen woman—a loathsome monument of the wrath of Him whose vivid lightning is a passing shadow compared to his glance when once he is angry. She trembled and wept, while the Lawgiver prayed for mercy. The Lord refused to hear till the judgment had impressed the offender, and the entire multitude with its fearful lesson. For seven days she was an exile from the camp; and in their yet unshaken regard, the host waited uncomplainingly for her return. What days of meditation and repentance to the erring Miriam! Genius had been to her as beauty to the wives of the patriarchs, a dangerous gift—and on the dizzy eminence of Power, she forgot her frailty, and the homage due to Jehovah.

In the desert of Zin, Miriam died. The people in all their tents sent up the notes of wailing for the dead, till the dark defiles of girdling summits were filled with the solemn echoes, and Canaan itself seemed to have vanished forever from the horizon of hope. The maiden-prophetess was dear to her wandering and weary nation. They had heard the story of her watching with breaking heart in her girlhood by the flowing Nile—they had seen her by the Red Sea, beneath the rolling mist of returning billows, stand like a rejoicing angel, and strike her timbrel to the Lord, pouring her chorus of victory upon the ear of solitude, and over the deep grave of the on-rushing foe! They buried her at the base of a lonely height, whose tower of granite, is a fit memorial of her lofty genius, and singular pre-eminence as the first female ruler and prophet mentioned in the sacred record. The shadow it flings upon her grave, might remind the beholder of the blemish that darkens her memory, and its gilded top pointing Heavenward when evening has shrouded the plain, indicate the character and destiny of the illustrious sleeper!

Paul refers to the history of Moses as illustrating the power of faith. It was confidence in the promise of God, that in spite of perils which made the effort to save his infant life like waiting at the sepulchre's mouth, committed him to Miriam and the Nile. It was the same trust, breathed in Jochebed's counsels and prayer, that cheered the sweet maiden while she loitered among the reeds, and started at the plunge of the crocodile from his banquet of babes. It was faith that made her worthy to stand with the brotherhood in the Red Sea's wave, and look calmly on its up-rolling waters. It was faith, *woman's* faith triumphant, that shouted victory amid the desert's gloom and the thunder of the boiling deep, till the sound reached the very top of Heaven. And finally, faith was by her side with a convoy of angels and chariot of fire, when the last struggle came on in the vale of Paran—and she turned her fading eye in love on the white tents of Israel, while the recollection of her sin, which like a dark cloud had spent its wrath upon her shrinking form and retired, rushed upon her spirit from the luminous past.

So is woman's destiny identified with that of the church of the Living God. More than once the ark of his covenant has rested upon her shoulder, and she has folded to her bosom the whole interests of Zion in peril; leaning as the very "Bride of Christ," when all others had fallen, meekly yet heroically upon the arm of her Beloved.

DEBORAH

Bethel, now called Beiten by the wandering descendants of disinherited Ishmael, lies in a solitary valley among the mountains twelve miles north of Jerusalem.

Here Jacob rested on his way to Padanaram, and while he slept in sadness and weariness, beneath the open sky, had a beatific vision of the worshipping train that fill the "Temple not made with hands." Wh n he arose he poured the consecrating oil, and named the place Bethel, "the house of God." It was here he buried Deborah, who had long been an inmate of his family, distinguished for her kindness and piety. In this solitude the ark and tabernacle had rested in sacred seclusion. But it also became the very fastness of Judean idolatry, and the heights which had glowed with the presence of God, were darkened with the shadow of temples to Ashtaroth and Baal. The defiles which had echoed the thrilling voice of the Eternal sent back the shouts of licentious revelry, and the blasphemies of idol-worship.

Grieving over this desolation in Israel, and expostulating with her countrymen, there was Deborah the Prophetess, Judge among her people. According to Eastern custom she pitched her tent in summer in the shade of a spreading palm, and gave judgment upon the lawless, uttering in their reluctant ears the gathering wrath of the Lord for their guilty alienation from him. They were crushed by the despotism of a heathen invader, and their fruitful fields were turned into a desert. With oblations they crowded the shrines that glittered on every summit, while the scourge fell more heavily, and the cry of distress arose more wildly with their increasing apostasy.

Deborah devoutly trusted in God, and knew that deliverance would follow rebuke. She remembered the flood, when a lonely vessel with a single family rode the crest of the billows amid the drifting dead, proclaiming to the universe that "the Lord's portion is his people." She read the same sublime truth, in promises to the patriarchs and their rescue from the vengeance of foes, and it was felt in every answer to prayer. Calling Barak, commander of the national forces, she assured him the country was ripe for insurrection—that Jehovah would shake the throne of Jabin, and vindicate his own sullied honor by tarnishing the glory of an oppressor, whose nine hundred chariots of iron and vast army, encompassed them darkly as the horizon of despair. Barak was skeptical, and hesitated to assume the commission; but told Deborah if she would attend him, he would rally his scattered bands and hazard the desperate encounter. Girding on his sword, with the prophetess he entered his chariot and drove with tempest-speed along the valleys, summoning the tribes around the drooping standard of Israel. Jabin was reposing luxuriously in his palace by Lake Merom when the news of revolt and revolution reached his ear. He curled his lip in scorn, and told his brave General, Sisera, to harness his steeds to his scythed chariots, and as a pastime of war ride over the restless

Hebrews till the flame of rebellion was extinguished in blood. Barak with ten thousand men marched up the side of Mount Tabor to its fortified top, and watched their coming, the thunder of whose myriad wheels shook that mountain, over whose stillness hovered the wings of the Almighty, and the angel of victory waved unseen the banner of a celestial host! Deborah looked off on the scene, with the eye of a poet and prophet. On the north lay the valleys and mountains of Galilee. Towards the south, was the wide plain of Esdrelon, guarded on one hand by Mount Hermon, and on the other by Gilboa. Eastward, Kishon, "that ancient river, Kishon," wound among the hills to the Mediterranean, whose waters melted away into the haze of the horizon. On the west, slept in the sunlight the sea of Genesareth, and Jordan rolled its waves. Nature was peaceful and glorious—as though the sweet vale of Kishon could never tremble to the tread of slaughtering armies, and its current be turned by the slain into a torrent of blood.

The host of Sisera came pouring down the defile into the plain, when Deborah raised her shout—"Up! Barak! for this is the day in which the Lord hath delivered Sisera into thy hand; is not the Lord gone out before thee? Barak with his ten thousand soldiers then made a descent to the banks of the river, where the Canaanites, numbering according to Josephus three hundred thousand footmen and ten thousand cavalry, were drawn up in battle array.

Sisera stood in his chariot and surveyed his legions with their flying banners, caparisoned steeds, and Captains impatient for the glory of conquest, and turned with a glance of haughty contempt toward the steady march of his unequal foe. With a shout that was heard along the enemy's line like a trumpet-call, Barak's columns dashed into the very bosom of Sisera's host, led on by disciplined horsemen, and walled in by chariots of iron which sent a tempest of javelins, and the slinger's hail of death; while swords clashed and gleamed in the resistless onset of the Hebrew battalions. The imperial ranks were broken, and reeled before the shock. Sisera rallied his hitherto invincible forces, and swept down upon the enemy like an engulfing tide—and again recoiled before the steady and deadly advance of the undrilled army, Deborah had called into being, like Rhoderic's men, uprising with flashing steel from the brakes of the mountain slope. He turned to flee, and the soldiers followed in dismay before the devouring sword into the current of Kishon, to pass over. But the waters which often rose suddenly from the swollen streams of the summits at its source, overflowed the banks, and they were borne, a shrieking and ghastly throng, with horses and chariots, weapons, and ensigns of battle, down beneath the surging and crimson flood. Deborah and Barak, like Moses and Miriam, looked on the scene, and gave God the glory. Behold, in the distance, the fugitive chieftain of that Gentile host! Barak pursuing, now catches a glimpse of his flying form on the crest of a hill, and again he is lost from his straining sight.

Heber, a descendant of Jethro, had pitched his tent in the plain of Zaanaim, and maintained neutrality during the fierce contest which restored the independence of Judea. His wife saw Sisera coming, and with a cheerful salutation offered him the refuge and hospitality of her home. The terrified and weary man turned in to rest till the pursuer had passed. She spread over him a mantle, and calmed his fears as the shout of the enemy came faintly to his ear, and he looked wildly through the parted curtains on the path of his flight. Jael bade him repose securely, and he fell asleep; for the struggle of that burning day and escape from the battle-field, had overtasked his frame and bewildered his thought. Stealing quietly to his pillow, with a single stroke, the iron entered his throbbing temples, and fastened him to the earth. A convulsive start, a look of agony, a tremor of his manly form, a gasp for life, and all was over—the dew of the sepulchre was on his brow, and his long locks lay clammily round his pallid features and rayless eye, which just before shone with heroic fire in the deepening conflict. Then came Barak flushed with victory, and Jael met him. She told him to go in and look at the man he was pursuing;

and with his hand on his sword-hilt, he entered the tent to complete the slaughter. But *a woman*, according to Deborah's prediction, as a reproof for his own timidity, has snatched the laurel from his extended hand. Starting back from the corpse her blow had riveted to the ground, with wounded pride, he gazed silently on his helpless foe. The cloud hung but a moment upon his noble spirit; he thanked God, applauded the Kenite for her deed, and bore the body in triumph to the foot of Tabor, where the prophetess had beheld the scene of battle, and waited his return.

Then sang Deborah and Barak, a duet of great sublimity; a song through which runs a seraphic ardor—a holy panting of soul to emulate in praise those who pour their tide of harmony into the depths of eternity! Every cliff and defile of Mount Tabor echoed the melody, and the forest seemed to shake its green leaves with joy, while the anthem died away on the bosom of distant Carmel. The multitude stood mute and motionless, as the jubilant strains rose like the sky-lark's song to Heaven's gate, then descended in fainter tones as if a wail for the dead, to the bed of the slain.

Oh! little thought they then, that the mountain-top on which they encamped, and which now stood a monument of mercy and of wrath, would, in the lapse of ages, become more luminous than day beneath the opening sky, while Moses and Elias descended in their white robes to commune with the transfigured Son of God, whose brightness fell on the astonished disciples, till they bowed and worshipped in fearful reverence. Now did they deem that on its consecrated brow, a mighty Homicide would stand and pour his troops upon the same trampled plain. That when the strife was over, and the smoke of the battle gathered upon the still height while dying groans went sadly up its side, the shout of blasphemy and the riot of lust, would rent the air and fill with the cries of fiends its hallowed solitude.

Deborah returned to the shade of her Palm Tree, and Israel to the High Places, and shivered the idols of Baal. Whether we contemplate this gifted woman listening to the complaints of her people, and uttering her decisions with the dignity and authority of a Judge—or attended by Barak sounding through all the coast the tocsin of war; standing on Mount Tabor, and gazing unterrified on the living tide of armed men —or with the conqueror when the battle was past, in the utterance of purest poetry giving all the glory to God, she commands equally our admiration. This is the second heroine in Scripture invested with princely power, and gains in the comparison with Miriam. For if she had faults, they are unrecorded, and she stands before us unblemished by the homage of a grateful nation, who, in their devotion, added to her titles that of Mother in Israel.

How impressively the scenes at which we have glanced illustrate the fact, that earth is a sphere of probation and trial, foreshadowing in its retributions, the scenes of that day when every man will reap the harvest he has sown. The chastisement of the Hebrews—the overthrow of their persecutors in turn—the fall of Sisera, and the affection Deborah received as a more valued reward than laurels, for well-doing when the popular taste was wholly against her; are replete with encouragement and warning, and point to the decisions and the doom of a final adjudication.

JEPTHA'S DAUGHTER.

THERE is a tragical interest in the brief story of Jeptha's Daughter. It contains the elements of physical, mental, and moral suffering, which have power over the imagination and the heart.

Jeptha a Gileadite, was an illegitimate son, and consequently subject to galling insults and cold neglect, which strongly marked his character. He became an independent, impetuous and fearless man, whose daring exploits won distinction for the youthful hero.

This enhanced the hostility of his brethren, until they banished him from the ancestral domain, and appropriated to themselves his patrimony. He fled to the land of Tob, beyond the frontier of Israel, probably in the borders of Arabia, and supported himself in his solitude, by depredations upon the enemies of his people, a career not forbidden by the ethics of those primitive days. His achievements soon gathered around him a band of lawless men—a company of brigands ready for the wildest onset, or the dark and patient vigil

" Of him who treasures up a wrong!"

"Even our different climate and manners afford some parallel in the Robin Hoods of former days; in the border forays, when England and Scotland were ostensibly at peace; and in principle, however great the formal difference—in the authorized and popular piracies of Drake, Raleigh, and the other moral heroes of the Elizabethan era."

Jair, the judge in Israel at the time of Jeptha's expulsion, died, and the Hebrews, yielding to that strange tendency of the human soul toward idolatry, because in his absolute personality Jehovah is invisible, introduced the forms of image-worship which met their observation in all their intercourse with the tribes that hung menacingly upon their boundaries. The loss of influence and dignity, disloyalty to God carried along with it, besides the withdrawment of his protection, invited the hordes of idolaters to conquest—and like the northmen who poured resistlessly upon the plains of degenerate Italy, the Amorites on one side, and the Philistines upon the other, overswept the land.

Then the Jewish Elders turned to Jeptha, whose prowess alone could rally his inefficient and suffering countrymen. His reply to the delegation who found him in his fastness among the desolate hills exhibits the spirited independence of the fugitive. "Did not ye hate me, and expel me from my father's house? and why are ye come to me now, *when ye are in distress?*" They conciliated the chief by offering him the generalship of the army. He accepted on condition as security against permitting again his banishment, while he was also conscious of his ability to govern, that if victorious, he should be made Judge in Israel. That he was not an unprincipled bandit, is evident from his tactics in the projected war. He personally demanded of his foes the ground of their invasion; and when they asserted their original claim, he laid down an acknowledged principle in the law of nations, that the actual possessors of the land when taken by the Israelites, conferred a full and unquestionable title.

The negotiation closed, and the opposing armies prepared for battle. Then appeared the religious element in the character of Jeptha, however obscured before, in a solemn vow, altogether rashly spoken. He pledged to the Lord, if he would overthrow the legions of Amorites and allow him to return a conqueror peacefully to his dwelling, the first living form he met as a burnt-offering upon the altar of thanksgiving. It strikes one, from the fact his home was cheered by a loving and only daughter, he must have apprehended the possibility of her welcome upon his triumphant return—but in the brilliant prospects before him and his bleeding country, with the weight of responsibility so unexpectedly assumed, his enthusiasm and the doubtful struggle before him, absorbed all considerations of personal sacrifice, and gave no time for deliberation.

Girded with his tried sword, he led his army from the declivities, across Jordan where the enemy blackened the plain, and sent out their loud challenge to conflict. The might of the Lord came upon him, as on Barak the son of Abinoam, and he dashed like a falling bolt into the ranks of gleaming spears and waiting blades. They closed around Jeptha's bands, then reeled and rallied, and again fell back as a forest before the hurricane, till the rout was complete. But Jeptha followed up the victory till twenty cities capitulated, and his weary soldiers refreshed themselves in the valley of vineyards, whose soil was reddened by the lifeblood that flowed in the trenches, with trodden clusters from the overshadowing vine.

Then followed the trial and the offering. With a guard of his grateful warriors he marched towards Mizpeh—and "Behold, his daughter came forth to meet him with timbrels and with dances; *and she was his only child.*"

In his wanderings and loneliness, *she* had been true, and lived in the smile that played upon his stern features when by his side, and had wept when sadness subdued the wonted brightness of his flashing eye. He had thrown around her from his strong arms in the affection of a great yet wounded heart, and twined in musing fondness her ringlets around the hand that foemen feared. And now more beautiful than ever, in the fine excitement of filial rapture, with a train of damsels who had gathered at the tidings of conquest to celebrate the splendid career of her father, she approaches him with a salutation in which was poured a tide of joy that spoke through every lineament of her lovely face. The fear that had made his brain reel at times along the way, was merged in the crushing certainty of a terrible reality. Rending his robes, he cried, "Alas! my daughter—for I have opened my mouth unto the Lord and I cannot go back."

When the rush of new emotion that met the subsiding swell of gratulation, as the gloomy surges of a sudden tempest chase the sunlit-billows, was passed, and a mournful calmness succeeded, she stood there a touching monument of early piety and disinterested love, neither romance nor the pages of profane history can furnish. Then she said, "My father, if thou hast opened thy mouth unto the Lord, do to me according to that which has proceeded out of thy mouth; forasmuch as the Lord has taken vengeance for thee of thine enemies, the children of Ammon." Then pausing, while he was mute in the dread paralysis of grief and remorse, she asked the delay of two months in the execution of his vow, while attended by her companions, she went forth upon the solitary mountains to bewail her virginity.

There the doomed maiden wandered like the very spirit of solitude, beamed a sky that seemed to mock her destiny with its cloudless glow, and reposed at night while the changeless stars beamed brightly, as when she strayed blithely there with the exiled Jeptha. The months vanished, and she returned with uncomplaining fidelity to yield her life upon the sacrificial altar.*

Curiosity is left to conjecture in regard to the particulars of that last parting of Jeptha and his daughter—his fruitless lament while she hung upon his neck, and

---

* When the circumstances and evidences are carefully considered, the opinion that she was *sacrificed* " according to his vow" rests on the strongest probability, nor would, it is believed, be questioned, were it not for the fearful result it involves.

her soothing accents of cheerful resignation. And when she lay in robes of virgin purity upon the altar, and closed her mild eye, while the high-priest lifted his burnished blade, what an illustration of the authority of conscience, that brought her there, and which echoes unceasingly when unperverted, the claims of immutable right. It has a whisper more awakening than the trumpet-blast—and a power that invests a man with the majesty of an angel, or the dark sublimity of a demon.

The scene also illustrates the solemnity of covenant obligation to the Christian, and its eternal force. The individual consecration, and baptismal vow to train offspring for God, compared with Jeptha's hasty and criminal oath, are infinitely more fearful—and inscribed on the columns of the White Throne, will meet the gaze when "this mortal shall put on immortality."

WERE Life, like the "Court of Death," thrown on canvass, it would be no less a picture of contrasts—a panorama of visible scenes and shades of character dissimilar ever, though perpetually changing. In the market-place, the incarnate fiend jostles the humble saint—the haughty rich man passes with scorn the unoffending poor. The vile walk unblushingly by the side of the virtuous, glorying over innocence and beauty blasted forever; and the weak cower beneath the frown and grasp of the strong. In the forum, the unworthy judge gives sentence on the less guilty criminal, and the citizen of unstained integrity sits on the same jurors' bench with the undetected villain. The statesman, the orator, and the bard, crowned with honor and weary of praise, lie raving with delirium, or in idiotic silence before the intoxicating bowl; and the proudest prince, and the hero of a thousand battles, kneeling in unresisting captivity, cast crown and laurels at the feet of beauty. Such a contrast as the last has distinguished Delilah among the women of Scripture memory, while by the portraits already drawn, she forms one no less striking as a female character. She was a beautiful Philistine, living on that border of Canaan settled by the tribe of Dan.

Samson, son of Manoah, who like Isaac

was the gift of God in answer to prayer, became judge over his nation harassed by enemies, about forty years after Jeptha's death. Of remarkable strength and daring, he was great unlike any before him. Barak, Gideon and Jeptha, led brave armies and obtained splendid victories: Samson was *an army in himself*, and hurled defiance by the might of his single arm at the hosts of Israel's foe. In one of his excursions to Philistia he saw Delilah, and admired her beauty. The valiant judge had occasion often afterward to visit the valley of Sorek, and at length made the damsel his bride.*

The lords of the Philistines saw that Samson was in the toils of love—that a syren's voice had well nigh drowned the call of duty and the mandate of "The un-

---

* His marriage is not mentioned, but as commentators differ on this point, I have chosen the supposition that Delilah was his wife.

known God." They therefore went to Delilah with flattering persuasion and a bribe of money, to induce her to extort from him the secret of his strength, and deliver him into their hands.

Three times he made a pastime of her curiosity, and when she thought he was her captive, swung his sinewy arms in mock-endeavor to escape, and walked away from his thraldom with a smile of triumph wreathing his lip. But as often as she met him, with chiding fondness Delilah would fix her dark eye upon him, and throwing around him all the fascination of voluptuous loveliness, entreat him to tell her the talisman of his strength.

Harassed with the affairs of state, he sought her home to refresh his drooping spirits, and as often was wearied with her request, till one day reclining by her side, and completely under the influence of her charms, he told her his long and raven locks were the badge of his might—the glory of the Nazarene. God had made this the symbol of his miraculous *relation* to Him, and he threw it as a toy into the lap of the Gentile beauty. He fell asleep on her knee, and calling a Philistine she bade him shave off the luxuriant hair that lay in folds upon his brawny shoulders; then cried, "The Philistines be upon thee, Samson!" He awakened, and starting at the repeated alarm, shook his noble frame, and took the wonted attitude of battle with his foes. But Jehovah who was his strength had abandoned the victor. Despoiled of his eyes, he was led to Gaza, whose gates he had once borne away at night, and loaded with chains of brass.

It is not probable Delilah anticipated this result, but only expected his temporary confinement. Milton has so beautifully delineated in "Samson Agonistes" both the hero and his wife, we shall introduce extracts from the scene of their meeting, just before he was led from the mill where he had toiled as a national slave, to entertain with his feats thousands of the populace and nobility assembled in the great temple of Dagon, worshipping there before his shrine, and holding a jubilee to commemorate the brilliant achievement of the champion's capture.

Delilah goes sorrowfully to the lonely captive, yet admired of the multitude as she sweeps by with an air of royalty—

> Like a stately ship
> Of Tarsus, bound for th' isles
> Of Javan or Gadire,
> With all her bravery on, and tackle trim,
> Sails fill'd, and streamers waving,
> An amber scent of odorous perfume
> Her harbinger, a damsel train behind.
> * 　 * 　But now, with head declin'd,
> Like a fair flower, surcharg'd with dew, she weeps,
> And words address'd seem into tears dissolv'd,
> Wetting the borders of her silken veil.

DELILAH.

Delilah attempts to conciliate Samson, expressing her sorrow over the unlooked-for consequence of her folly, and desire to atone, if possible, for the fearful act.

SAMS.—Out, out, hyæna! these are thy wonted arts,
And arts of every woman false like thee,
To break all faith, all vows, deceive, betray,
Then as repentant, to submit, beseech,
And reconcilement move with feign'd remorse,
Confess, and promise wonders in her change.

*   *   *   *   *

DEL.—Yet hear me, Samson; not that I endeavor
To lessen or extenuate my offence,
But that, on th' other side if it be weigh'd
By itself, with aggravations not surcharg'd,
Or else with just allowance counterpois'd,
I may, if possible, thy pardon find
The easier towards me, or thy hatred less.
First granting, as I do, it was a weakness
In me, but incident to all our sex,
Curiosity, inquisitive, importune
Of secrets, then with like infirmity
To publish them, both common female faults:
Was it not weakness also to make known
For importunity, that is for naught,
Wherein consisted all thy strength and safety?
To what I did, thou show'dst me first the way,
But I to enemies reveal'd, and should not;
Nor shouldst thou have trusted that to woman's frailty:

Ere I to thee, thou to thyself was't cruel.
Let weakness then to weakness come to parl,
So near related or the same of kind,
Thine forgive mine. * * *

SAMS.—How cunningly the sorceress displays
Her own transgressions to upbraid me mine!
* * * Weakness is thy excuse,
And *I believe it;* weakness to resist
Philistia's gold; if weakness may excuse,
What murderer, what traitor, parricide,
Incestuous, sacreligious, but may plead it?
All wickedness is weakness: that plea therefore
With God or man will give thee no remission.

Delilah then interposes the plea of importunity from her countrymen, and religious obligation urged by the priest of Dagon.

SAMS.—I thought where all thy circling wiles would end;
In feign'd religion, smooth hypocrisy.

DEL.—I was a fool, too rash and quite mistaken
In what I thought would have mended best.
Let me obtain forgiveness of thee, Samson,
Afford me place to show what recompense
Towards thee I intend for what I have misdone,
Misguided. * * * *
I to the lords will intercede, not doubting
Their favorable ear, that I may fetch thee
Forth from this loathsome prison house to abide
With me, where my redoubled love and care

DELILAH.

With nursing diligence, to me glad office,
May ever tend about thee to old age,
With all things grateful cheer'd, and so supplied,
That what by me thou hast lost, thou least shalt miss.

S<small>AMS</small>.—No, no, of my condition take no care;
It fits not; thou and I long since are twain;
Nor think me so unwary or accurst,
To bring my feet again into the snare
Where once I have been caught : I know thy trains,
Though dearly to my cost, thy gins and toils;
Thy fair enchanted cup and warbling charms
No more on me have power; their force is null'd,
So much of adder's wisdom I have learn'd
To fence my ear against thy sorceries.

* * * * *

D<small>EL</small>.—Let me approach at least and touch thy hand.

S<small>AMS</small>.—Not for thy life, lest fierce remembrance wake
My sudden rage to tear thee joint by joint.
At distance I forgive thee ; go with that,
Bewail thy falsehood, and the *pious works*
It hath brought forth to make thee memorable
Among illustrious women, faithful wives.
Cherish thy hasten'd widowhood with the gold
Of matrimonial treason! So farewell.

D<small>EL</small>.—I see thou art implacable, more deaf
To prayers than winds and seas; yet winds to seas
Are reconcil'd at length, and sea to shore :
Thy anger unappeasable still rages,
Eternal tempest never to be calm'd.
Why do I humble thus myself, and, suing

For peace, reap nothing but repulse and hate!
* * * * *
Fame, if not double-faced, is double-mouth'd,
And with contrary blast proclaims most deeds;
On both his wings, one black, the other white,
Bears greatest names in his wild airy flight.
My name perhaps among the circumcis'd,
In Dan, in Judah, and the bordering tribes,
To all posterity may stand defam'd,
With malediction mention'd, and the blot
Of falsehood most unconjugal traduc'd.
But in my country where I most desire,
In Ecron, Gaza, Asdod, and in Gath,
I shall be nam'd among the famousest
Of women sung at solemn festivals,
Living and dead recorded, who to save
Her country from a fierce destroyer, chose
Above the faith of wedlock bands; my tomb
With odors visited and annual flowers;
Not less renown'd than in Mount Ephraim
Jael, with inhospitable guile
Smote Sisera sleeping, through the temples nail'd.
Nor shall I count it heinous to enjoy
The public marks of honor and reward
Conferr'd upon me, for the piety
Which to my country I was judg'd to have shown.
At this whoever envies or repines,
I leave him to his lot, and like my own.

Whether Delilah was in the mighty structure when Samson was the sport of his captors—the subject of scorn and brilliant wit by the nobility of Philistia—we cannot tell. She may have stood sad and silent with remorse, and remembered kindness she would share no more, while leaning mournfully between the massive pillars he grasped with extended arms, he bowed his sightless head and prayed for the return of his forfeited power, that he might avenge his own, and the enemies of God. It is in accordance with God's retributive justice on former occasions, to believe she was there, and when in answer to that piteous cry of a penitent spirit, the tall columns reeled before his recovered strength, like interlocking masts in a wrathful deep, and the walls heaved and fell in with the descending roof, her's was the first shriek that went up from that vast tomb of living throngs, whose music and mirth were drowned in a wail of agony and groans of the death-struggle.

This wonderful man, a greater than Hercules, was evidently subdued by his affliction, and a loyal worshipper of God—with all the strange contradictions in his character, his inglorious fall and tragical death, he joined without doubt, the patriarchal ranks above; while the fair idolater clung to her gods and perished forever.

Previous to her advent, the women of Bible fame, pass before the imagination in the vision of antiquity, like pure and radiant stars, their frailties scarcely more than the wing of a transparent cloud upon these beautiful spheres. Delilah rises suddenly from darkness, as a glorious meteor describes an arc of romantic and fatal light, and goes down in an horizon of awful gloom. Beauty with an unsanctified heart, no less than intellect, is a bright *anathema*—and while others mourn its bestowal, the possessor is ultimately a wreck, over which angels weep!

THE story of Ruth, written doubtless by Samuel, and thrown in between the desolating wars of the Judges and those which followed under the Kings, is a touching picture of quiet pastoral life—a lifting of the curtain rolled in blood, from the *background* of tragic scenes, upon a peaceful home, where love has its trial and triumph. The thoughts rest like the Dove upon a green hill-top, after flying wearily over the unburied slain and a deluged world, upon this bright vision amid heathen cruelties and slaughtered armies. We could not spare the short book of Ruth from the Bible. It not only illustrates God's particular providence and protection of his people, but is an indispensable link in the genealogy of Christ, and is thus quoted in Matthew. A Moabitess is united to the ancestry of David, foreshadowing the truth that the Redeemer would shed his love and recovering mercy on the Gentile nations.

Voltaire dwelt with enthusiasm on the marvellous sweetness and simplicity of this "gem in oriental history."

Fiction has never written so truthful and beautiful a tale—one while it reaches and subdues the heart, leaves no stain that would soil an angel's purity. Like all God's works and manifestations, it is faultless.

"No novelist has ever been able, with

his utmost efforts, to paint so lovely, so perfect a character as this simple story presents. From first to last, Ruth appears before us endowed with every virtue and charm that render a woman attractive. Naomi's husband was a man of wealth, and left Bethlehem to escape the famine that was wasting the land. In Moab he found plenty, and there with his wife and two sons, who married Ruth and Orpah, lived awhile and died. In the course of ten years, the two sons died also, and then Naomi, broken-hearted, desolate and poor, resolved to return and die in her native land. How touching her last interview with her daughters-in-law, when she bade them farewell, and prayed that as they had been kind to her and her dead sons, so might the Lord be kind to them. Surprised that they refused to leave her, she reasoned with them, saying that she was a widow and childless, and to go with her was to seek poverty and exile in a strange land. She could offer them no home, and perhaps the Jewish young men would scorn their foreign birth, and when she died none would be left to care for them or protect them. There they had parents, brothers, and friends, who loved them and would cherish them. On the one hand were rank in society and comfort, on the other disgrace and poverty. Orpah felt the force of this language and turned back; but Ruth, still clinging to her, Naomi declared that it was the act of folly and madness to follow the fortunes of one for whom no bright future was in store, no hope this side the grave. She sought only to see the place of her childhood once more, and then lie down where the palm trees of her native land might cast their shadows over her place of rest. 'Go back,' said she, 'with my sister-in-law.' She might as well have spoken to the rock:—that gentle being by her side, all shrinking timidity and modesty, whose tender feelings the slightest breath could agitate, was immovable in her affections. Her eye would sink abashed before the bold look of impertinence, but with her bosom pressed on one she loved, she could look on death in its grimest forms unappalled. Fragile as the bending willow, she seemed, but in her true love, firm as the rooted oak. The hand of violence might crush, but never loosen her gentle clasp. With those white arms around her mother's neck, and her breast heaving convulsively, she sobbed forth, '*Entreat me not to leave thee*, for where thou goest I will go, and where thou lodgest I will lodge: thy people shall be my people, and thy God my God: where thou diest I will die, and there will I be buried:— *naught but death shall part us.*'

"Beautiful and brave heart! home, and friends, and wealth, nay, the gods she had been taught to worship, were all forgotten in the warmth of her affection. Tearful yet firm, 'Entreat me not to leave thee,' she said; 'I care not for the future; I can bear the worst; and when thou art taken from me, I will linger around thy grave till I die, and then the stranger shall lay me by thy side!' What could Naomi do but fold the beautiful being to her bosom and be silent, except as tears gave utterance to her emotions. Such a heart outweighs the treasures of the world, and such absorbing love, truth and virtue, make all the accomplishments of life appear worthless in comparison.

"The two unprotected women took their journey on foot towards Bethlehem. It was in the latter part of summer, and as they wandered along the roads and through the fields of Palestine, Ruth by a thousand winning ways endeavored to cheer her mother. Naomi was leaving behind her the graves of those she loved, and penniless and desolate, returning to the place which she had left with a husband and two manly sons, and loaded with wealth, and hence a cloud hung upon her spirit. Yet in spite of her grief she was often compelled to smile through her tears, and struggled to be cheerful, so as not to sadden the heart of the unselfish, innocent being by her side. And at fervid noon, when they sat down beneath the shadowy palm to take their frugal meal, Ruth hastened to the neighboring rill, for a cooling draught of water for her mother, and plucked the sweetest flowers to comfort her.

"Thus, day after day, they travelled on, until at length, one evening, just as the glorious sun of Asia was stooping to the western horizon, the towers of Bethlehem arose in sight. Suddenly a thousand tender associations, all that she had possessed and all that she had lost, the past and the present rushed over her broken spirit, and she knelt and prayed and wept. 'Call me not,' said she to the friends of her early days, who accosted her as she passed through the gates, 'call me not Naomi, or the pleasant, but Mara, *bitter*, for the Almighty has dealt very bitterly with me.'

"Here again Ruth's character shone forth in its loveliness. She was not one of those all sentiment and no principle; in whom devotion is mere romance, and self-sacrifice expends itself in poetic expressions. Though accustomed to wealth, and all the attention and respect of a lady of rank, she stooped to the service of a menial in order to support her mother. With common hirelings she entered the fields as a gleaner, and without a murmur trained her delicate hands to the rough usage of a day-laborer. At night her hard earnings were poured with a smile into the lap of her mother, and living wholly in her world of love, was unmindful of everything else. Boaz saw her amid the gleaners, and struck with her modest bearing and beauty, inquired who she was. On being told, he accosted her kindly, saying that he had heard of her virtues, her devotion to her mother, and her self-sacrifices, and invited her that day to dine at the common table. With her long, dark locks falling in ringlets over her neck and shoulders, and her cheek crimsoned with her recent exertions, and the excitement at finding herself opposite the rich landlord, in whose fields she had been gleaning, and who helped her at the table as his guest, sat the impersonation of beauty and loveliness. That Boaz was fascinated by her charms, as well as by her character, was evident. He had watched her deportment, and saw how she shunned the companionship of the young men who sought her acquaintance, and of whose attentions her fellow-gleaners would have been proud. Nothing was too humble, if it ministered to her mother's comfort, but beyond that she condescended to nothing that was inconsistent with her birth. Whether abashed by his looks and embarrassed by his attentions, or from her native delicacy of character, she arose from the table before the rest had finished, and retired. After she had left, Boaz told the young men to let her take from the sheaves without rebuke, and then, as if suddenly recollecting how different she was from the other gleaners, and that every sheaf was as safe where she trod as it would have been in his own granary, he bade them drop handfuls by the way, which she, wondering at their carelessness, gathered up. At sunset she beat it out and carried it to her mother. Naomi, surprised at the quantity, questioned her closely as to where she had gleaned, and when Ruth told her the history of the day, the fond mother divined the whole. Her noble and lovely Ruth had touched the heart of one of her wealthy kinsmen, and she waited the issue.

"The long conversations they held together, and the struggles of the beautiful Moabitess, before she could bring herself to obey her mother and lie down at the feet of Boaz, thus claiming his protection and love, are not recorded. Custom made it proper and right, but we venture to say that Ruth never passed a more uncomfortable night than that. Her modesty and delicacy must have kept her young heart in a state of agitation that almost mocked her self-control. The silent appeal, however, was felt by her rich relative, and he made her his wife. The devotion to her helpless mother—her self-humiliation in performing the office of a menial—the long summer of wasting toil—the many heart-aches caused by the rough shocks she was compelled, from her very position, to receive, at length met with their reward. Toiling through the sultry day, and beating out her hard earnings at night, the only enjoyment she had known was the consciousness that by her exertions Naomi lived. It had been difficult, when weary and depressed, to give a cheerful tone to her voice, so as not to sadden her anxious mother-in-law; but still the latter saw that the task she had voluntarily assumed was too great, and therefore, at length, claimed from Boaz the obligations of a kinsman. Love, however, was stronger than those claims, and he took Ruth to his bosom with the strong affection of a generous and noble man. She thus rose at once to the rank for which she was fitted, and in time the beautiful gleaner of the fields of Bethlehem became the great-grandmother of the King of Israel."

Ruth was naturally affectionate and amiable, but evidently owed that moral elevation of character which made her decision to go with Naomi, although a forlorn hope even did not brighten their path, sublime in its unyielding strength, to the religious culture of that Hebrew mother.

Orpah, less deeply impressed with the worship of the living God, returned at the urgent entreaty of Naomi, to her wealthy friends, and the adoration of Chemosh, the deity of Moab.

There is a fine appeal to the moral feelings in the last address to Ruth. "Behold thy sister-in-law is gone back unto her people, and unto her gods; return thou after thy sister-in-law." In her deep distress, Naomi knew not what to do—and throwing all the responsibility on the weeping Ruth, seemed to say, "Before us is famine and death—you can avoid sharing this bitter cup by a return to your people and idols." With the spirit of a martyr that lovely being sobbed while she hung on Naomi's neck, "I cannot forsake thee—let thy fate and God be mine."

So did the family of Elimelech on the border of extinction, emerge from gloom into splendor which shines onward through all the lineage of David, blending at length with the glory that illumined the same vale of Bethlehem, when the chorus of angels was poured on the midnight air, because their King was cradled there in homeless solitude.

In a rich valley of Mount Ephraim, a central range of summits in Palestine, Elkanah, a pious shepherd, kept his flocks. As Jacob before him he married two wives, and had also to bear the curse which attends a violation of the law of marriage as it came from Heaven.

Peninnah had sons and daughters, while Hannah, unblest with children, was the most tenderly loved—the Rachel of his heart and home. Otherwise, there was nothing peculiar or remarkable in the quiet life of these dwellers among the mountains. Tracing their history, we seem returning to the patriarchal age—or rather looking in upon some "Cotter's Saturday Night" in the Highlands of Scotland. Every year, he went with his family on a pilgrimage to Shiloh, near Bethel, where the Ark and Tabernacle gathered for sacrifice and worship, the devout Hebrews from all their plains. Hannah was a meek and saintly woman, but Peninnah was vain and haughty. Her jealousy was kindled by Elkanah's attention to his more amiable wife, and glorying in her offspring, treated scornfully her childless rival in his affections. This grieved Hannah's sensitive spirit during their lonely travel to Shiloh, and yearning for the honor and joy of a mother, she would have knelt in her sorrow under the very wings of the Cherubim overshadowing the Mercy-Seat.

Upon one of these annual visits, tempted and heart-broken, she wept till Elkanah touched by her tears endeavored to soothe her with assurances of his own deep affection. Unlike the petulant Rachel, she uttered no reproach, but restraining her grief, lifted the gloom from his brow with a smile mournful as a gleam of sunshine on a solitary ruin. Then she sought the threshold of Jehovah's Temple, and bowed in silent prayer. The depths of her being were stirred, and wrestling with the Merciful One, she breathed a solemn vow that if a son were given her, he should be a consecrated child, and with the stern discipline of a Nazarine prepared for perpetual service in the Lord's House. Responsive to her intense emotion, her quivering lips only moved. Eli, who was sitting by the door-post of the Sanctuary, marked her strange deportment, and hastily misjudging, accused her of *drunkenness*. No murmur was heard from this resigned and humble worshipper, but in sad and melting accents, she said, "No, my lord, I am a woman of sorrowful spirit; I have drunk neither wine nor strong drink, but have poured out my soul before God." Eli was affected, and with altered tone replied, "Go in peace : and the God of Israel grant thee thy petition thou hast asked of him." Hannah felt that she had prevailed in prayar, and her countenance became tearless and hopeful. When the morning broke on the hills, gilding the gorgeous Tabernacle, the family arose and worshipped once more toward the symbols of the "Upper Sanctuary," and the flaming Law pencilled on the tables of eternity; then striking their tent, journeyed to Mount Ephraim.

And a son was born, named by Hannah,

Samuel, *asked of the Lord.* I know not of a more sublime manifestation of faith and piety, than her refusal to go up to the yearly festival until he was old enough *to be left there,* according to her vow, the living sacrifice of an earnest and grateful heart. Her religious principle was unbending as Paul's ages after, and the glory of God filled as vividly and constantly the horizon of her thoughts.

She went at length to the Holy Temple, with an oblation from the flocks and fields. The priests laid a slain bullock upon the altar, and while the smoke ascended, she took from the bosom that cradled him with unutterable tenderness the wondering babe, and gave him to Eli, saying, we might believe half in reproof, " O my lord, as thy soul liveth, my lord, I am the woman *that stood by thee here* praying unto the Lord. For this child I prayed; and the Lord hath given me my petition which I asked of him: Therefore also I have lent him to the Lord: *as long as he liveth* he shall be lent to the Lord." The venerable priest accepted the consecration, and with a solemn benediction devoted Samuel to the service of the Tabernacle.

Then Hannah uttered a prayer, which is rather a lofty ascription of praise to the Almighty, whose sovereignty exalts the beggar, while he shivers the sceptre and sinks the throne of a king. Kindling with rapture she emulates Deborah in celebrating His majesty, till the poetic fire mounts like a seraph's hymn to the unseen "Holy of Holies." Doubtless Eli understood keenly the allusion of that forceful expression, "The Lord is a God of knowledge, and *by him actions are weighed.*"

This mother, upon whose history it is sweet to linger, is the first woman mentioned in the Bible kneeling in the *attitude* of prayer—not because others were prayerless, but to fill out the delineation of maternal character and duty, of which Hannah is a model of singular excellence. She had the glow of enthusiasm and the composure under trial, of an intellect finely balanced, and disciplined by much communion with God.

Samuel grew, and bore through all his illustrious career, the most distinguished of judges and honored of prophets, the impress of that moulding influence, continued in kind by the man of God, by whose side he trimmed the temple-lamps and read the mysterious tablets traced by the finger of the Eternal.

Oh! what power is lodged in a mother's hand—what eloquence in her prayer, and what pathos in her tear! She can lead her child to the very gate of Paradise—and pour into the golden censer waved by the Angel before the Majesty on High, the incense of her petition. Her tear will burn through life on the brow it baptized, and the pressure of her hand be felt when the world itself has become a vanished dream. And many in that day, when Christ shall "come to make up his jewels," will point to the deepening glory that spreads away to the mount of God, and murmur—

> "A mother's holy prayer,
> A mother's hand and gentle tear
> Have led the wanderer there!"

The mild administration of the Judges had passed away. The splendor of the regal period of the Hebrews had reached its meridian; and the fame of Solomon attracted to his court a distinguished visitor— "The Queen of the South."

The land of Sheba was the Happy Arabia of the ancients, and is the Sabæa and Araby the Blest of modern poets. The present name is Yemen. It is the south western division of Arabia, and embraces an area equal to the whole of New England and New York. In contrast with the rest of Arabia, it has always been distinguished for fertility, beauty, and mineral richness. Especially has it been famous for gums, perfumes, and spices. "Neither," says the sacred record, "was there any such spice as the Queen of Sheba gave to Solomon;" and in our own day, her country is equally supreme in the excellence of its Mocha coffee. If the region was not the mine, its cities were, of old, the great marts also of precious stones and of gold, two hundred pounds of which were included in the gift of the queen to the king of Israel. It abounds in the palm, orange, apricot and sycamore; the hills are, and doubtless were, cultivated to their tops in terraces, and by means of artificial reservoirs; the valleys and water-courses are exceedingly luxuriant; the wilder parts are haunts of the antelope, gazelle, leopard, and tropical birds; and, like all Arabia, it has always been the home of that "living ship of the desert"—the camel, and that "glory of Arabia"—the horse. The adjacent seas are filled with superb shells; and the Persian Gulf on the one hand furnishes the finest pearls, the Red Sea on the other the most beautiful corals of all the world.

It was in this country, which, as Milton says, in his picture of Paradise,

>   ———"To them who sail
> Beyond the Cape of Hope, and now are past
> Mozambic, off at sea north-east winds blow
> Sabean odors from the spicy shore
> Of Araby the blest;"

—it was in this land, described in Lalla Rookh as the clime where

>   ———" Glistening shells of ev'ry dye
> Upon the margin of the Red Sea lie;
> Each brilliant bird that wings the air, is seen;—
> Gay, sparkling loories, such as gleam between

> The crimson blossom of the coral tree,
> In the warm isles of India's sunny sea;
> And those that under Araby's soft sun,
> Build their high nests of budding cinnamon;

—it was in this kingdom, and in some palace whose halls, and domes, and

> ———"towers,
> Were rich with Arabesques of gold and flowers,"

that the Queen of Sheba, whose name is Balkis in the Arabian traditions, was born and grew, and was crowned with the sovereignty of Happy Arabia.

No description of her person is given in the inspired history. It is enough to know that she belonged to a race that is regarded as supplying the "primitive model form—the standard figure of the human family." Baron de Larrey, surgeon-general of Napoleon's army in Egypt, said of the people of this same region—the east side of the Red Sea—"Their physical structure is, in all respects, more perfect than that of Euro-

QUEEN OF SHEBA.

peans; their figure robust and elegant; their intelligence proportionate to that physical perfection." Some of the glowing portraitures in the Song of Solomon, indeed, are supposed to have been drawn from his fair and royal visitor, so that we may infer that she realized a modern bard's picture of her later countrywomen:

> "Beautiful are the maids that glide
>   On summer eves, through Yemen's dales,
> And bright the glancing looks they hide
>   Behind their sedan's roseate veils."

But we have better proof that she had better qualities than beauty. It is one of the perfections of the Bible, that it compresses into a few words the whole biography and character of many individuals. Thus we are only told that Enoch "walked with God, and was not; for God took him;" and, in the Gospels, we hear of a poor woman who cast "all her living" into the treasury. In these hints, we have, as it were, the entire history of a godly man, and of a poor, pious woman. So, in the brief notices of the visit of queen Balkis, her intellectual and moral traits are clearly intimated—her early life readily suggested. The whole case is conveyed in our Saviour's language: "She came from the uttermost parts of the earth, to hear the wisdom of Solomon." In the Book of Kings, are further data. We see her lively and paramount interest in religion, when it is said, "she heard of the fame of Solomon, concerning the name of the Lord;" her disposition at once to recognize and worship the true God, in her words, "Blessed be the Lord thy God, which delighted in thee, to set thee on the throne of Israel forever; because the Lord loved Israel forever, therefore made he thee king to do judgment and justice"—the last words suggesting, also, her own upright character. Her proficiency in knowledge is indicated in the confident purpose "to prove" the wise man "with hard questions." Her frankness and earnest solicitude to learn, are evident from the declaration that "she communed with him of all that was in her heart," words that likewise discover to us her long, careful retention of subjects of inquiry. Her interest in household and architectural matters, is recorded; and so candid and appreciative was she, that "there was no more spirit in her." That she had too much sound sense to credit every floating report, is manifest from her refusal to believe the rumors of the king's acts and wisdom, until her eyes had seen them; that she was modestly disposed to acknowledge an error from her assurance that she had been mistaken; that she found her highest happiness in mental and moral improvement, from her exclamation, "Happy are thy men, happy these thy servants, who stand continually before thee, and that hear thy wisdom." Happy thy servants!—in how slight estimation did she clearly hold all rank and social position, when she thus envied the condition of menials who yet enjoyed so rare intellectual opportunities. And, to crown the whole delineation, the energy of her character is transcendently illustrated in the journey itself—a journey equivalent to a tour half around the globe, in these days; a journey of twelve hundred miles in a direct line, and much further in the winding course of travel; a journey over mountains, and unbridged rivers, and wide, trackless deserts, where the lion prowls, the scorpion stings, the simoom sweeps in scorching power, clouds and pillars of sand threaten the traveller, and fierce robbers hover around him; a journey of two months in going and two in returning, and if made, as it presumably was, in company with the merchant caravan that is known to have wintered in Sheba and spent the summers in Canaan, one that obliged her to be absent the greater part of a year from her dominions.

It is pleasant to trace, in imagination, the ingenuous, thoughtful youth of the Arabian Queen, her enterprising maturity, the surprises and delights of her visit, and the benefits of it, resulting to her nation, after her return. She had been educated with royal care, in all the learning of her country; yet she felt that her education was not finished—that she had much to learn. Her mind was busy with higher themes than dress, amusements, daily news, and earthly love; her soul no longer slept in the animal life of the senses—of sights and sounds, however refined; it had awakened to a deep feeling of, and a restless longing after, the True, the Good, the Beautiful, the Eternal. The crown, the sceptre, were hers, and she might have contented herself with princely pomp, with display of authority, with woman's alleged desire to rule; but this was not enough for her. The treasures of the kingdom were hers, and she could command in profusion the pearls and corals of the sea, the gold of Africa, the jewels of India, the fine linen of Egypt, the purple of Tyre, the silks of Persia; she might, like many others, have satisfied herself with costly raiment and equipage; but these were insufficient. Any eastern prince would have been made happy by her hand, and she could have at once retired into the seclusion of domestic delight, leaving the cares of state to her officers; but no, she was conscious of higher objects of existence than merely to be well wedded— we say, to be so, for her inquiring mind is evidence of her youth, and the silence of sacred writ, under the circumstances, is proof that she was a virgin queen. And all the luxuries of the land and the delicacies of the sea, were at her disposal; yet she could not feed her immortal soul with the ashes of pleasure, nor expend her whole intellect in royal entertainments. It was not permitted her to dance, for to this day, the dignified orientals esteem that exercise appropriate only to slaves and hirelings; but she could hire the waltzing maids of neighboring Abyssinia, with their tamborines and tinkling bells; yet she had a higher purpose of life than amusement, although, without doubt, she was as keenly sensible to the delights of music and motion, as was Coleridge in his dream, when, as he says,

> "A damsel with a dulcimer
> In a vision once I saw;
> It was an Abyssinian maid,
> And on her dulcimer she play'd,
> Singing of Mount Abora."

Queen Balkis could have further tried to slake her soul's thirst with the romances and legends that bloom so abundantly and gorgeously in the rich soil of Arabian imagination; and perhaps she tried, and failed to satisfy herself with these. Last of all, from her many courtiers and officers and subjects, she could have drank in flattery, and lived on the breath of praise.

After all, there was something awake and sleepless in her spirit. Those things in her heart, of which she afterwards communed with Solomon, were yet unexplained; the hard questions she subsequently put to him, were then unanswered. She felt her responsibility as a ruler, and her duty to fulfil her lofty sphere, and longed for wiser instruction in law and equity and political economy, than she had yet received. She had heard vague reports of the western nations, especially of the miraculous progress of the Israelites, and she wished to hear of their history, and that of other kingdoms. She looked upon the various vegetation and animal life of the earth, and desired to listen to some one who, like Solomon, could " speak of trees, from the cedar that is in Lebanon even unto the hyssop that springeth out of the wall; and of beasts, and of fowl, and creeping things, and of fishes." She gazed on the moon and stars, and felt that there was a higher wisdom to be drawn from them than the fancies of eastern astrology. She thought of life, and, to her, it was all a bewildering mystery; the perpetual questions stirred within her, From whence do I come?—whither do I go? And then she meditated on death and the dark unknown beyond, and doubted not there was something to be learned besides the sensual heaven of Arab poets, or the transmigration of the Egyptian and Hindoo.

She pondered concerning the Powers that created and rule the world, and dreamed of a higher and holier Power than the genii and gnomes and fairies of oriental romance, or the gods of mythology. A quenchless' flame of thought and feeling was lit in the warm heart and daring soul of Balkis, Queen of Araby the Blest.

And now as a lively trade sprang up between Jerusalem and Sheba, and caravans came and went, and the ships of Solomon sailed up and down the Red Sea, increasing information was diffused in Happy Arabia; the sailors and merchants then, as now, brought to unknown regions, reports of their country, religion, and government. They were summoned to the presence of the queen, and spoke of the amazing wisdom and glory of their monarch, of their national history, and of the one true and holy Jehovah. Perhaps, by some chance, they brought manuscripts of the books of Moses and of Solomon, and these deeply studied, fanned the curiosity of the queen, and enlightened and enlarged her mind. However it was, her decision was finally and resolutely formed. She knew the wearisome length and appalling dangers of the journey; but her determination was announced; the government was entrusted to the hands of her premier; the choicest gems, gold and spices were selected for her gifts; her retinue of soldiers and servants equipped and mounted, and the march commenced, the queen herself borne in a sedan, or throned in a canopied shade on a camel, or, her clear olive face veiled from the tropical sun, she mounted her favorite Arab horse, and dashed forward in the van. Sixty nights, her pavilion was to be pitched, and sixty mornings, to be struck again, before she reached her destination.

She saw the verdure of her own elysian land disappear, and came upon the sterile soil of Hedjaz, or Stony Arabia, the Red Sea all the while lying upon the left, and porphyry Mountains on the right. After thirty days, she came to the half-way halt —the present Mecca, where, in those days, or soon after, stood a temple with three hundred and sixty images, now supplanted by the Kaaba of the Mahometans. Then she passed the burning springs, surrounded with perpetual vegetation; next, the present Medina, now the place of the Prophet's tomb, with its four hundred columns and three hundred lamps, constantly burning. In a few days, Mount Sinai and Horeb rose to view, and the sovereign gazed in wonder at their shadowy summits, recalling the rumor of their memorable scenes. Here, her company crossed the hills of Arabia, struck upon the barren desert, and passed

Petra—the City of the Rocks, which then resounded with busy life, and stood in all its architectual freshness, not, as now, the haunt of the bat and serpent. At last, the Dead Sea was passed, the Jordan forded, the fields and vineyards of Canaan entered. How refreshing was the luxuriance of the land of milk and honey, after the dreary and fearful passage of the desert! The southern caravan came in the spring, and it was therefore late in the season when, in the familiar words of Solomon, "the winter is past the rain over and gone; the flowers appear on the earth; the time of the singing of birds is come, and the voice of the turtle dove is heard in the land. The fig-tree putteth forth her green figs, and the vines with the tender grape, give a good smell." It is probable that the King went forth some distance to meet his royal visitor, and if so, it may explain the words in his song: "Who is this that cometh out of the wilderness like pillars of smoke, perfumed with myrrh and frankincense, with all powders of the merchant?"

Thus did the queen of the South come from the uttermost parts of the earth, to hear the wisdom of Solomon. She came to the Mount of Olives, and as she passed it by the same road so often travelled by our Saviour on his way to Bethany, the prospect of Jerusalem, throned on its hills, broke in beauty upon her sight. There, in full view, like a scene of magic, was the temple-front, its porch, or tower, rising two hundred feet above the top of Mount Sion; there were Solomon's palace, the Queen's palace, the house of the forest of Lebanon, the porch of judgment; and both temple and palace, porch and pinnacle, so glittering with gold, so studded with pillars, rich in carvings of cherubim, lions, palm-trees, and flowers, varied with the purple, yellow and white of cedar and fir, that the whole resembled a scene which outrivals the gorgeous wealth of the East—a scene which this queen was never to behold—an American forest in the splendors of October. Gazing at the glories of Mount Sion, she crossed the brook Kedron, and was received at the palace with royal honors.

The main incidents during the visit are given in the sacred narratives. The highborn guest saw the arrangements of the palace; the royal table, to supply which for one day, required thirty oxen and two hundred sheep, besides deer and fowl; the two hundred targets, and three hundred shields, and various vessels, all of gold; the ivory throne, with its twelve carved lions; the thousand chariots and twelve thousand horsemen; the gardens of spikenard and saffron, pomegranates and cinnamon; the "orchards planted with all kinds of fruit," and beautiful with "fountains and pools of water;" and the massive stone walls, built up from the valleys to support the temple, some of the immense blocks remaining to this day. She heard the singers and the "musical instruments of all sorts." To the temple, she was not admitted; but we are told that she saw the ascent by which the king went up thither; and possibly, through the gates and doors, she may have distantly seen the brazen sea, and the glory of the Lord, filling the holy place.

Above all, she heard the wisdom of Solomon. From his own lips she heard some of those "three thousand proverbs, and a thousand and five songs," spoken of by the sacred writer. She put all her hard questions—communed of all that was in her heart. Doubtless the conversation was not made up of wit and dalliance, and the compliments of courtesy; nor did they talk alone of fashion, idle news, and the weather. The king was not obliged to treat her as an unthinking being, but rather driven to exert all his intellect to answer her inquiries into the great matters of law, history, science, and religion. Such a journey was not undertaken for nothing. The Redeemer had declared expressly that she "came to hear wisdom"—would that this was more often the object of travel and of conversation.

How long she remained is not stated. If, as already assumed, she came with the great merchant caravan, she may have staid two months in Canaan, and may have visited other places. "She turned, and went to her own country." That her visit resulted in good to her nation, as well as to herself, we have some evidence. We find, from history, that one hundred and sixty-seven years before Christ, the patriotic and pious Maccabees propagated a pure religion more readily in Sheba than elsewhere, and that the people were morally superior to the rest of the Arabians. Thus, more than eight hundred years after the death of this queen, there was a happy state of things in her country, which, it is fair to suppose, originated in her wisdom, energy and piety. It is the crowning praise of this crowned woman, that, in all probability, she faithfully discharged the high duties of her sphere, benevolently communicated her knowledge to her subjects, and fulfilled the mission of her life.

Aside from her energy, the two grand features of the character of Queen Balkis, as developed in the inspired history, are her mental activity and religious inclination. Like the two immense columns of brass, ornamented with pomegranates and chain-work, that stood in front of Solomon's temple, these intellectual and spiritual tendencies were the noble pillars of her character, around which all her lighter graces of soul were wreathed. These capabilities, diligently cultivated, prepared her to fulfil the lofty purpose of her existence. And it is in the power of every high-minded woman to be a queen, and wield a sceptre of influence as potent as the literal sceptre of the sovereign of Happy Arabia. Nor has the young American woman now to come from the ends of the earth, to hear the wisdom of the wise. All knowledge is within her reach, and she is raised to the dignity of the equal and companion of man. Nor is there any danger that, under a true cultivation, she will neglect more appropriate duties in higher aspirations. Woman's sphere is just that circle of influence which she can fill without the neglect of her special offices, though it be a world blessed by her benevolent aid, or instructed or delighted by her thought. And to fill this, her powers need not be obtrusively exerted; her authority, whether asserted or not, will be in exact proportion to her intelligence and moral force of character; and a silent but powerful influence will necessarily go out from her, as the Arabian queen, perfumed with myrrh and frankincense, and bearing costly spices, everywhere on her journey made the desert air rejoice in the balmy breath.

JEZEBEL was a Sidonian princess of commanding figure, vigorous intellect, and depraved heart. Like Delilah, she was a voluptuary and an idolater.

Ahab, king of Israel, a man of weak mind and utterly destitute of moral principle, from a motive of policy similar to that which controls matrimonial alliances among the sovereigns of Europe, or influenced by her personal attractions, made her his queen.

Her genius soon gave her the ascendency over him and in the cabinet of his kingdom. In the temples of Ashtaroth and Baal, she had bowed with the enthusiasm of a devotee. She kissed the hideous images of her gods with burning lip, and breathed their names with the reverence and consecration of a martyr. And when she rode to the capital of Israel, and saw on the hills and house-tops no altars but those of the golden calves of Dan and Bethel, symbolical of the Living God, with the silent energy of an independent spirit, conscious of its power to rule, her purpose was formed to revolutionize the ancient religion of the Hebrews, and in the very Tabernacle of the Shekinah, kindle the flame of sacrifice to the sun-god—Baal.

The festivity and civic display attending her reception at court passed by, the acclamations of the people ceased, and her work was begun—this resolute propagandist of idolatry, who resembles Lady Macbeth in the great and revolting qualities of her character, was imbued with the sentiment of the invocation of that illustrious homicide.

> ———" Come, come, you spirits,
> That tend on mortal thoughts, unsex me here;
> And fill me from the crown to the toe, top-full
> Of direst cruelty! make thick my blood,
> Stop up the access and passage to remorse;
> That no compunctious visitings of nature
> Shake my fell purpose, or keep peace between
> The effect and it."

The prophets were the first victims of her malignant cruelty, and were slaughtered till only a hundred were left, who were concealed by the good Obadiah, governor of the royal household. From the fact that no more mention is made of them, it is evident they were at length dragged forth by the executioners of her hostility to the worship of Jehovah, although its celestial glory was already gone, and its hallowed rites had given place to the forms of prevailing superstition.

Elijah, gifted and fearless, was especially the object of Jezebel's hatred. He lived awhile by the brook Cherith, near Jordan, a solitary hermit, mysteriously fed by ravens, till the approaching footsteps of the messengers of death perilled his life. The Lord then sent him to the house of a poor widow in Zidon, whose table he miraculously supplied, and raised her only son from the dead. One day, when Obadiah, by the command of Ahab, was surveying the land to find a gushing spring or green spot for the flocks perishing in the famine with which God had cursed the nation, Elijah met him, and told him to inform the king of his abode.

The monarch, goaded on by the unwasting zeal of the queen, went forth to slay his enemy. But the prophet hurled back his bitter reproaches, until he stood pale and cowering beneath the eagle eye of his accuser; and then proposed to go with him to Mount Carmel, where, in the presence of his pagan priesthood, the authority of Baal against that of God should be fairly and finally tested. Like the dark waves which clasp the summit they are submerging, the thousands of Israel crowded up the lofty mountain to behold the scene—for fire from Heaven was to descend on the altar of the Lord, or his homage be transferred forever to the idols of Jezebel.

The four hundred and fifty priests erected their altar, and called on Baal till their cries were one wild shriek, and cut their flesh till the trenches ran with blood; but there came no consuming shaft from the skies—no voice of approval stilled the wailings of the frantic worshippers. Then Elijah built the despised altar of Jehovah, laid the slain victims thereon, and flooding the whole with water, gathered the excited throng around it. The god of the sun had given no answer but the steady blzae which withered the fields and made the starving millions living skeletons. Now in lonely majesty the hunted prophet knelt in prayer, " and lo, fire from the cloudless heavens fell like falling lightning, and the bullock smoked amid the water that flooded it, and a swift vapor rose from the top of Carmel, and all was over." Then arose the swelling shout, " The Lord he is the God ; Jehovah he is God !" The prophets of Baal were massacred in the valley below, turning the waters of Kishon in to a crimson flood. The people dispersed in the silence of an unearthly fear, and Elijah went back to the brow of Carmel to pray for rain.

While Ahab tarried for refreshment, the

march of the tempest came to the prophet's listening ear, and he sent his servant to hasten the king's flight to Jezreel. Elijah, strengthened by the might of the Lord, wrapped his mantle about him, and girded his lions, while the wrathful clouds blackened above his dauntless form like a descending robe becoming his dignity, and ran before the foaming steeds of Ahab, to the gates of the city.

He thought Jezebel could not fail to believe now the king had bowed before the God of Israel, and been dazzled with the glance of his omniscient eye. She listened proudly and unmoved to the story of her trembling lord, then sent a messenger to Elijah, threatening with an oath, to mingle with the corpses of her priests, his own body, before the evening of another day. He fled to Beersheba, and his unrelenting persecutor, bewailing the dead, effaced with raillery and scorn from the heart of Ahab, any impression the miracle may have made, chiding him till he was ready to sue for pardon, for his *weakness* on Mount Carmel.

And soon after, when he wanted the vineyard of Naboth, a citizen, to extend his gardens, but could not prevail on him to part with the ancestral possession, he went in tears to the palace, and throwing himself on his couch refused to eat. Jezebel heard his complaint, and gazing upon him with a glow of indignation, and the fierce passions of a tigress, she said contemptuously, "Dost thou not govern the kingdom of Israel? Arise, and eat bread, and let thy heart be merry: *I* will give thee the vineyard of Naboth, the Jelzeelite." Faithful to her promise, she wrote letters in the name of Ahab, and with the royal seal, sent them to the elders of the city and the nobles, commanding them to proclaim a fast, and arraign Naboth for blasphemy against "God and the King." False witnesses were suborned, and the mock trial soon closed. The victim was taken out of the city and stoned to death. The remorseless queen then told the king to confiscate the vineyard, for the owner would trouble him no more. He went down accordingly, but while walking over the grounds, Elijah crossed his path, forewarning him of his death, on the very spot where Naboth died at the hands of a lawless mob. Conscience, though it slumbered deeply, always awoke at the sound of Elijah's voice—and he exclaimed in blended anger and anguish, "Hast thou found me, O mine enemy?" Then followed a terrible prediction of the entire destruction of his family, and the tragical end of Jezebel.

Ahab was fatally wounded not long afterwards in a battle with the Assyrians, and died; the prophet ascended in a chariot of fire to glory, and his mantle with " a double portion of his spirit," fell on his companion Elisha, who was to be an actor in the last scene of this doomed dynasty. He anointed Jehu, a captain in the army of the king, to execute the hastening vengeance of God. The host rallied around his standard, and blew their trumpets in joyful acclamation, while he led them on towards the walls of the capital. Meeting Joram son of Jezebel the reigning sovereign, and Ahaziah her grandson, king of Judah, who came forth in their alarm at the sight of that war-cloud, sweeping as on the wings of a hurricane along the hills, he pierced the former with an arrow, and throwing the body into the vineyard of Naboth, slew the other in his chariot, and dashed on to the open gate of Jezreel. The shouts of the populace, and the rushing of chariot-wheels, reached the chamber of the queen.

No time was demanded, no weeping for the slain disturbed her Satanic self-command. Painting her face, and splendidly attired, "she looked out at the window," and calling to Jehu, reminded him of the fate of Zimri the conspirator against Elah, who perished in the flames of the palace, his own hand kindled. Jehu looked up and cried to the eunuchs, "Who is on my side?" The quick reply was the descending form of Jezebel, mangled on the projecting wall, and sprinkling the horses with blood. He then drove over this dying daughter of a king, and queen of Israel, stern, sullen and daring to the last, till the hoofs of his steed were red with trampled dead.

Entering now the desolate palace-hall, he told the throng to go and "see this cursed woman, and bury her, for she is a king's daughter." But in accordance with prophecy, they found only the fragments of Jezebel's body left by the dogs. Jehu continued his work of slaughter till the idolatrous race was extinct, and the dishonor cast on the name of Jehovah was wiped out with the blood of a whole generation.

Woman may be grateful for the seclusion that brings with it the culture of her sympathies and moral sensibilities; and that she is excluded from manifold temptations that crowd the pathway of man, whose restless eye turns ever to the height, however distant, whereon stands the temple of Mars, Jupiter, or Mammon; inviting him to come with the sacrifice of principle and the hope of Heaven, and take

> "The wreath of glory that shall burn
> And rend his temples in return."

For with the same opportunity and urgency of motive, she would oftener enroll her name among the great, whose power blasted where it fell, and whose fame rose with the commission of gigantic crimes.

THE family of Ahab is among the most impressive illustrations in history, of maternal influence for evil on the character of offspring. The nefarious Jezebel not only gave birth to Athaliah, but laid a shaping hand on her destiny; and evidently with a sibyl's enthusiasm, opened before her youthful feet the very *descensus Averni* in the mysteries of crime, hitherto unknown in royal annals. We have no biography of her early years; her career of dissipation and bursts of passion while a maiden, within the magnificent walls of her father's palace.

The pious Jehosaphat, who reigned in Judah, strangely sought her hand for his son Jehoram. No other motive can be imagined than the policy of kings, who live in jealousy or fear of each other. And when her husband, yet a youth, took the sceptre, she threw around him the magical power of her wiles, and put forth the guiding energy of genius—a force, which under the mad rule of passions, like the sun-chariot in Phæton's hand, makes ever a brilliant, disastrous and brief career; and,

"Self-stung, self-deified,"

is overtaken by the retributive thunderbolt, at last.

One after another, Jehoram's five brethren, who held posts of honor in the kingdom, and others of the nobility, disappeared suddenly under the assassin's stroke, or poison administered by Athaliah, until he sat in solitary and sullen authority, on a throne behind which was "a power greater than itself."

Naboth's history had furnished a precedent the queen was not unwilling to follow, and the tragedies in both branches of an impious line, remind us of the Borgia family of modern history, who have written their names in blood, on the ecclesiastical and civil records of Italy. The king was smitten with disease, and after lingering for two years, till a loathsome spectacle to his friends, died, and left the crown to Ahaziah.

This son, unlike his predecessor, was not involved in the suicidal war with a conscience made tender by the piety of a father, but with pliant docility listening to the dark counsels of Athaliah, was striding onward in power that spared neither Jewish altar, nor the form of a rival, when, during a visit to Joram, he was slain at Jehu's command, with the retinue that escorted him to Jezreel.

This gradual extinction of her family did not move the lion heart of Athaliah. She resolved, with demoniac ambition, to strew around the summit of dreaded pre-eminence, the slain "seed royal," from the infant to the manliest youth; and firmly hold a sceptre dripping with the life current of her own household. The order was given, and, as she thought, the massacre complete, and, a gloomy despot, she could repose upon a throne whose shadow would terrify, while the sword that guarded it would cut for her a pathway whither a sublimely desperate will might guide her footsteps.

But she had a daughter, not yet insensible to human helplessness and the voice of love. Among the bodies of her brother's sons, which lay heaped together for interment, Jehosheba discovered the infant Joash, gasping for life, and secretly conveyed him to her chamber. For six years the child was hidden, and Athaliah reigned without a rival in the holy city.

At the expiration of that period, Jehoiada the priest, observing that the people were ripe for revolution, conferred with the centurions, captains and guards, and obtaining from them an oath of fidelity to his cause, showed them Joash in the house of the Lord. They had supposed the royal line extinct, and when they looked on the boy, who returned their caressing with shrinking wonder, old associations were revived, and many a veteran, who remembered the glorious days departed long ago, felt the quickening pulsations of slumbering loyalty, and his brow began to glow with an enthusiasm which seemed to have vanished forever.

The venerable priest then stationed the battalions at the principal gates of the Temple, and around the king, who stood in the bloom of his boyhood, half unconscious what all this preparation meant, encircled by a wall of men and gleaming weapons. Placing the crown upon his head, and the law of God in his hand, he poured on that fair forehead, the anointing-oil. Then the multitude " clapped their hands, and said, God save the king!" till the arches of the sacred edifice echoed back the acclamation, and the lofty columns rocked before the steady tramp of thousands, rushing to this scene of coronation.

The jubilant trumpets, and the deepening shouts caught the ear of Athaliah, and she hastened to the house of God. When she saw the splendid array and the surging waves of excited men, and the youth crowned in the midst of them, while " God save the king" rolled in a deafening chorus to the swell of trumpet blasts, her fallen glance read the truth that sealed her doom —and as a last struggle, she rent her flowing robes, and shouted, "Treason! Treason!"

But none flew to the rescue of the frantic queen. " Have her forth," cried Jehoiada, " without the ranges; and him that followeth her kill with the sword." The command was obeyed, and her body lay in the highway to the palace, trodden in the soil by the horsemen, who but a few hours before quailed before her eye of flame. Mother and daughter, alike in unblushing impiety which vaulted to the stars, perished equally wretched in their hurried and hopeless departure from a world they made more desolate, to an abode where Justice completes his work.

To what a towering greatness in guilt the intelligent creatures of God may attain! Those whom poets call angels, and who may be so amid the suffering

"On life's broad field of battle,"

become sirens on the shoals of ruin, or quaff with a smile of glorying the wine-cup of unmingled depravity.

And through all the history of the Hebrew nation, the lesson is enforced which Jehovah taught by the prophet, "*In my wrath I gave them a king*"—as if monarchy were a *dèrnier ressort* when the dignity of self-government was gone, and His image so nearly effaced from free intelligences, that the sovereignty is insufficient, which, "like the atmosphere we breathe, is felt only by resistance."

THE reflective reader of Scripture feels perhaps more deeply than the most logical array of argument, the inherent evidence of its inspiration. There is a singular and unequalled impartiality in its developments of character. Amid the atrocious adventures of kings, and the conspiracies of subjects—idolatry, war and pestilence—are exhibitions of unblemished authority, pure devotion, and glimpses of domestic fidelity and joy, which stamp the narrative with the seal of a faithful record. True to all experience is the picture drawn by the Holy Ghost, of earth and the immortal dwellers upon its surface. While *that* affirms a perfect creation and disastrous ruin, every observant eye beholds on all sides, strewn the fragments

"Of a temple once complete."

It was during the reign of Ahab, that the Shunamite, whose name with the "poor widow's" is unknown, left by her philanthropic deeds an imperishable memorial of her virtue.

Shunem was a city in the valley of Esdrelon, whose extensive plains were the scene of the most fearful conflicts in Jewish warfare, till its soil was moistened with blood; and the billows of waving grain, as on the field of Waterloo in modern time, told where the ridges of the dead had mouldered. Before this wealthy town, Saul encamped with his army on the eve of his last great battle.

It was, therefore, often the asylum of wounded and dying warriors of bordering nations; and its inhabitants had every opportunity for the exercise of mercy and kindness to the suffering. Among those who sought occasion for doing good, in the expansive spirit of pure benevolence, was a woman of fortune and influence. She met Elisha one day on his way to Mount Carmel, and gave him a pressing invitation to share the hospitality of her dwelling.

He accepted, and during the interview, there was awakened a religious sympathy and friendship, which continued ever after. In his travels through Shunem, he made her house his home.

Observing that the man of God was meditative and spiritual, with the consent of her husband, she furnished a little chamber expressly for his accommodation. By an Oriental seat, she placed a lamp that would burn all night; still a custom in the east when a guest is received with flattering attention. An English traveller not many years ago was thus entertained at the house of a Jew in Asia Minor.

That cheerful seclusion became dear to Elisha; and his raptures while prophetic visions made its walls a diorama of the future, will be known only,

> "When pictured on the *eternal wall*,
> The past shall reappear."

It was after a day of weariness of frame and of heart, he reached at eventide his favorite attic. The Shunamite heard his footsteps, and supplied his table, anticipating with wakeful interest all his wants. The next morning, contemplating her unwearied kindness, he was touched by the recollection of so disinterested love towards a homeless seer, and told his faithful servant to call her. He inquired what he could do for her in return.

The miracles he had wrought, made him a favorite at the royal court, and he offered to use his influence with the king and the captain of his host, in her behalf. He doubtless referred to an honorable position in the palace, or military aid and glory if desired, for her husband.

The reply displays her beautiful contentment with retirement—"I dwell among my people;" the cordialities of social life and the amenities of home, were all within the bright circle, ambition had drawn on "the sands of time." Thwarted in his purpose, Elisha consulted Gehazi, who suggested that no offspring beguiled the hours of the lonely Shunamite. He knew how the hope of forming at least a link in the lineage of the Messiah, to a Jewish wife, made a childless marriage doubly desolate. The prophet again sent for her, and moved by the unerring spirit, promised her a son. In the rush of emotion the announcement excited, and feeling the improbability of the event, she entreated Elisha not to mock her tears, for that hope had withered long ago.

He calmed her agitation, and renewed the promise. The child was born and grew up an idol by her side. Upon a summer day, he rambled into the harvest fields, where his father was at work with the reapers. His pastime among the sheaves, and his blithesome laugh, made the old man forgetful of his toil. Often pausing over the gathered grain, he watched the lad, while a smile passed like a gleam of light over his tranquil features.

But the sun blazed in a cloudless sky,

and beat on that tender brow, till it drooped as a stricken flower. His brain was on fire with pain, and passing his forehead with his little hands, he looked into his father's face and cried piteously, "My head, my head." He was carried to his mother, but nothing could revive his sinking form or retain the suffering spirit. At noontide he laid his head, like a wounded bird nestling under the maternal wing, upon her bleeding bosom, and died. She gazed awhile on the expressionless eye, and the face yet beautiful, over which the death-pallor was stealing, and then her thoughts flew to the man of God.

She went to Elisha's chamber, laid the corpse on his bed, closing the door gently, as if she might disturb that strange slumber, requested her husband to send immediately a young man and an ass. But he had given up for burial his dead boy, and thought her frantic grief had shaped this wild purpose of finding the prophet. With surprising self-command, she replied, "It shall be well," and vaulting into the saddle, bade her attendant to drive the animal to the top of his speed.

Elisha was on the summit of Carmel—the highest promontory on the coast of Palestine. It is mantled with foliage from its crown of whispering pines and lofty oaks, to the olive and laurel girdling its slopes with fruit and evergreen. Adown its sides, a multitude of crystal streams dance beneath interlocking boughs, to the sweeping Kishon, marching to the blue Mediterranean. It has a *thousand caves*, which have ever been the abode of prophet, recluse and monk. From its top, the view of the bay of Acre, with its fruitful shores—the blue peaks of Lebanon, and the White Cape, is enchanting.

The seer was looking off on this landscape spreading away on every side, in which the grand and picturesque view mingled in endless variety, and waiting for revelations from the fearful dome above to a bewildered world, when he beheld in the haze of a distant vale the hastening Shunamite. He told Gehazi to go down and meet her, and inquire if it were well with her family. With tearful resignation, she answered, "*It is well,*" and pressed upward to the eminence where Elisha sat. The servant deeming her an irreverent intruder on the hallowed solitude, held her back, till at Elisha's command, she was suffered to clasp his robe in anguish.

God, for some reason, had not informed the prophet of that domestic calamity.— With what delicacy and force she made known her affliction—said nothing of the child's sickness and death, but reminded him that when she desired the blessing it was with a request that he would not deceive her—as if it were more cruel than neglect, to press the cup of joy to her lips, and dash it aside—to relight the star of hope upon her solitary way, then blot it out forever.

Elisha understood the sad import of the appeal, and bade Gehazi go and lay his staff upon the face of the sleeper. But *a mother* was not so put off. She clung to Elisha, saying, "As the Lord liveth, and as thy soul liveth, *I will not leave thee!*" The servant, proud of the honor, ran and laid the staff on the dead—but there was no stirring amid the chords of the pulseless frame—no voice answered to his call.

The prophet entered the chamber alone, " and shut the door upon the twain"—the living and the dead. He knelt in prayer, then rose and stretched himself on the body.

Warmth returned faintly, and in his mental agitation, he strode with hurried step through the silent apartments of that house of mourning. Once more he embraced the corpse, and the luminous eye opened sweetly upon him, as when he turned in hither for reposing from the dust of travel, and met upon the threshold the laughing boy. The Shunamite was called, and when she saw again the wonted smile, and heard again the music of a harp that seemed unstrung forever, utterance was not equal to her full heart, and she sank at Elisha's feet. Then taking up her son with a clasping energy of fondness, none could know, unless like her they emerged from the shadows of the tomb, snatching from death's skeleton hand a loved one, she hastened to her husband; and Elisha went on his prophetic mission.

Years after, famine drove the Shunamite

to a foreign land. When she came back, her possessions were gone, strangers had effaced her title, and she was penniless. Just at this point of despair, Gehazi was conversing with the king respecting Elisha's miracles, and particularly the restoration of the dead in Shunem. When the houseless widow was proved by that servant to be the same for whom the marvellous deed was done, the monarch sent officers to restore her fortune; rendering at last through the prophet's popularity, the aid he apprehended she might need, when his gratitude was struggling to find expression.

Here we have the history of another noble mother, to whom the honor of God in daily life, and in the gift of offspring, was the central thought—the sublime principle of action, and sustaining power beneath the beatings of the storm that darkened her future.

And so God takes care of his trusting ones, who hold on to his extended hand when the surges rise, and the heavens are wild with the meeting clouds. It is then he often whispers peace, and the gloom is broken by gushing radiance from the rifted folds of the tempest—and the melody of a purer sphere fills the sky arching lovingly life's slumbering sea.

'The greatest events in human history awaken the least interest, because of their "quiet might." Men look at startling results, but lose sight of the sublime force of a cause which attracted no eye but God's. They behold the flying timbers and flaming ruins of a conflagration, but forget that the fearful power was concealed in a rising spark. A noble mind is wrecked, and many weep, but do not know that the blast which stranded the bark, was once the gentle breath of maternal influence, unhallowed by piety. So the splendid career of a hero and patriot, like Mordecai, Moses, or Washington, is less glorious than the simple *decision* made amid the conflicting emotions of youthful aspiration, to honor God and serve a struggling country.

Jehovah illustrates this principle in all his administration. What to Elijah on the solemn mount was the sweep of the hurricane, rending the cliffs and tossing rocks like withered leaves in air—the thunder of the earthquake's march—the blinding glow of the mantling flame—compared to the "still small voice" that thrilled on his ear, so full of God! It is not strange that there is to be a reckoning for "idle words" even, for they have shaken the world, and their echo will never die away.

The story of Esther, without an allusion to the fact, is a most beautiful illustration of this shaping of destiny by the interpretation of particular providence, in the commonest incidents of life. His church is saved from extinction, by events which appear accidental, and might not have happened for anything we can trace. The whole book is like a transparency hung before the pavilion of the Almighty, through which his counsels shine, and his unerring hand is visible.

Esther lived quietly with her kinsman Mordecai, who remained in Persia, when many of the captive Jews, during the reign of Cyrus, returned to their own land. Ahasuerus the king, to commemorate his victories and prosperous administration, extending from India to Ethiopia, and embracing a hundred and twenty-seven provinces, made a magnificent festival which continued six months. This was to display his power and wealth, before the nobility of his realm, and representatives from the conquered provinces of his spreading empire. At the expiration of this brilliant entertainment, he gave the common people, without distinction, a feast of seven days, in the court of his palace. The rich canopy and gorgeous curtains, with their fastenings—the tall columns, the golden couches, and tessellated floors—are described as "white, green and blue hangings, fastened with cords of fine linen and purple to silver rings, and pillars of marble: the beds were of gold and silver, upon a pavement of red, and blue, and black, and white marble."

Of this grandeur, amid the ashes strewn by wasting ages, are imposing remains. Modern travellers pause before "the vast, solitary, mutilated columns of the magnificent colonnades," where youth and beauty graced the harems of Persian monarchs.

Upon this occasion, the queen had a private pavilion for her female guests. But during the successive days of dissipation, the mirth waxed loud in the apartments of the king. The flashing goblet circulated freely, and his brain became wild with "wine and wassail." As the crowning display of his glory, Vashti in her jewelled robes and diadem, must grace the banquet. The command was issued, and the messenger sent. This mandate, requiring what at any time was contrary to custom, the appearance of woman, unveiled, in an assemblage of men, now when revelry and riot betrayed the royal intoxication, overwhelmed the queen with surprise. A thousand wondering and beaming eyes were upon her, during the brief pause before answering the summons. Her proud refusal to appear, roused the fury of Ahasuerus, already mad with excitement. It would not answer to pass by the indignity, for a hundred and twenty-seven provinces were represented at his court, and the news of his sullied honor would reach every dwelling in his realm, and curl the lip of the serf with scorn. The nobles fanned the flame of his indignation. Unless a withering rebuke were administered, their authority as husbands would be gone, and the caprice of woman make every family a scene of daily revolution.

Vashti was divorced—and to provide for the emergency, his courtiers suggested that he should collect in his harem, all the beautiful virgins of the land, and choose him a wife. Among these was Hadassah, the adopted daughter of Mordecai. He urged her to enter her name among the rivals for kingly favor. It was not ambition merely that moved Mordecai. He had been meditating upon the unfolding providence of God toward his scattered nation, and felt that there was deeper meaning in passing events than the pleasures and anger of his sovereign. Arrayed richly as circumstances would permit, the beautiful Jewess, concealing her lineage, joined the youthful procession that entered the audience chamber of Ahasuerus, where he sat in state, to look along the rank of female beauty, floating like a vision before him.

"The character of Esther is here exhibited at the outset; for when she went into the presence of the king, for his inspection, instead of asking for gifts as allowed by him, and as the others did, she took only what the chamberlain gave her. Of exquisite form and faultless features, her rare beauty at once captivated the king, and he made her his wife.

"Mordecai always reminds one of Hamlet. Of a noble heart, grand intellect, and unwavering integrity, there was nevertheless an air of severity about him—a haughty, unbending spirit; which with his high sense of honor, and scorn of meanness, would prompt him to lead an isolated life. I have sometimes thought that even he had not been able to resist the fascinations of his young and beautiful cousin, and that the effort to conceal his feelings had given a greater severity to his manner than he naturally possessed. Too noble, however, to sacrifice such a beautiful being by uniting her fate with his own, when a throne was offered her; or perceiving that the lovely and gentle being he had seen ripen into faultless womanhood, could never return his love—indeed could cherish no feeling but that of a fond daughter, he crushed by his strong will his fruitless passion. In no other way can I account for the life he led, lingering forever around the palace gates, where now and then he might get a glimpse of her who had been the light of his soul, the one bright bird which had cheered his exile's home. That home he wished no longer to see, and day after day he took his old station at the gates of Shushan, and looked upon the magnificent walls that divided him from all that had made life desirable. It seems also as if some latent fear that Haman, the favorite of the king—younger than his master and of vast ambition, might attempt to exert too great an influence over his cousin, must have prompted him to treat the latter with disrespect, and refuse him that homage which was his due. No reason is given for the hostility he manifested, and which he must have known would end in his own destruction. Whenever Haman with his retinue came from the palace, all paid him the reverence due to the king's favorite but Mordecai, who sat like a statue, not even turning his head to notice him. He acted like one tired of life, and at length succeeded in arousing the deadly hostility of the haughty minister. The latter however, scorning to be revenged on *one* man, and he a person of low birth, persuaded the king to decree the slaughter of all the Jews in his realm. The news fell like a thunderbolt on Mordecai. Sullen, proud, and indifferent to his own fate, he had defied his enemy to do his worst; but such a savage vengeance had never entered his mind. It was too late however to regret his behavior. Right or wrong he had been the cause of the bloody sentence, and he roused himself to avert the awful catastrophe. With rent garments, and sackcloth on his head, he travelled the city with a loud and bitter cry, and his voice rang even over the walls of the palace, in tones that startled its slumbering inmates.

"It was told Esther, and she ordered garments to be given him, but he refused to receive them, and sent back a copy of the king's decree, respecting the massacre of the Jews, and bade her go in, and supplicate him to remit the sentence. She replied that it was certain death to enter the king's presence unbidden, unless he chose to hold out his sceptre; and that for a whole month he had not requested to see her. Her stern cousin, however, unmoved by the danger to herself, and thinking only of his people, replied haughtily that she might do as she chose—if she preferred to save herself, delivery would come to the Jews from some other quarter, but she should die.

"From this moment the character of Esther unfolds itself. It was only a passing weakness that prompted her to put in a word for her own life, and she at once rose to the dignity of a martyr. The blood of the proud and heroic Mordecai flowed in her veins, and she said, 'Go tell my cousin to assemble all the Jews in Shushan, and fast three days and three nights, neither eating nor drinking; I and my maidens will do the same, and in the third day I will go before the king, and *if I perish, I perish.*' Noble and brave heart! death—a violent death—is terrible, but thou art equal to it!

"There, in that magnificent apartment, filled with perfume,—and where the softened light, stealing through the gorgeous windows by day, and shed from golden lamps by night on marble columns and golden-covered couches, makes a scene of enchantment,—behold Esther, with her royal apparel thrown aside, kneeling on the tessellated floor. There she has been two days and nights, neither eating nor drinking, while hunger, and thirst, and mental agony, have made fearful inroads on her beauty. Her cheeks are sunken and haggard—her large and lustrous eyes dim with weeping, and her lips parched and dry, yet ever moving in inward prayer. Mental and physical suffering have crushed her young heart within her, and now the hour of her destiny is approaching. Ah! who can tell the desperate effort it required to prepare for that terrible interview. Never before did it become her to look so fascinating as then; and removing with tremulous anxiety the traces of her suffering, she decked herself in the most becoming apparel she could select. Her long black tresses were never before so carefully braided over her polished forehead, and never before did she put forth such an effort to enhance every charm, and make her beauty irresistible to the king. At length, fully arrayed and looking more like a goddess dropped from the clouds, than a being of clay, she stole tremblingly towards the king's chamber. Stopping a moment at the threshold to swallow down the choking sensation that almost suffocated her, and to gather her failing strength, she passed slowly into the room, while her maidens stood breathless without, listening, and waiting with the intensest anxiety the issue. Hearing a slight rustling, the king, with a sudden frown, looked up to see who was so sick of life as to dare to come unbidden in his presence, and lo! Esther stood speechless before him. Her long fastings and watchings had taken the color from her cheeks, but had given a greater transparency in its place, and as she stood, half shrinking, with the shadow of profound melancholy on her pallid, but indescribably beautiful countenance, her pencilled brow slightly contracted in the intensity of her excitement—her long lashes dripping in tears, and lips trembling with agitation; she was—though silent—in herself an appeal that a heart of stone could not resist. The monarch gazed long and silently on her, as she stood waiting her doom. Shall she die? No; the golden sceptre slowly rises and points to her. The beautiful intruder is welcome, and sinks like a snow-wreath at his feet. Never before did the monarch gaze on such transcendent loveliness; and spell-bound and conquered by it he said in a gentle voice: "What wilt thou, Queen Esther? What is thy request? it shall be granted thee, even to the *half of my kingdom!*"

"Woman-like, she did not wish to risk the influence she had suddenly gained, by asking the destruction of his favorite, and the reversion of his unalterable decree, and so she prayed only that he and Haman might banquet with her the next day. She had thrown her fetters over him, and was determined to fascinate him still more deeply before she ventured on so bold a movement.

At the banquet he again asked her what she desired, for he well knew that it was no ordinary matter that had induced her to peril her life by entering unbidden, his presence. She invited him to a second feast, and at that to a third. But the night previous to the last, the king could not sleep, and after tossing awhile on his troubled couch, he called for the record of the court, and there found that Mordecai had a short time before informed him through the queen, of an attempt to assassinate him, and no reward been bestowed. The next day, therefore, he made Haman perform the humiliating office of leading his enemy in triumph through the streets, proclaiming before him, "This is the man whom the king delighteth to honor." As he passed by the gallows he had the day before erected for that very man, a shudder crept through his frame, and the first omen of coming evil cast its shadow on his spirit.

"The way was now clear to Esther, and so the next day, at the banquet, as the king repeated his former offer, she, reclining on the couch, her chiselled form and ravishing beauty inflaming the ardent monarch with love and desire, said in pleading accents, "I ask, O king, for *my life*, and that of my people. If we had all been sold as bondmen and bondwomen, I had held my tongue, great as the evil would have been to thee." The king started, as if stung by an adder, and with a brow dark as wrath, and a voice that sent Haman to his feet, exclaimed: "*Thy life!* my queen? *Who* is he? *where* is he that dare even think such a thought in his heart?" He who strikes at thy life, radiant creature, plants his presumptuous blow on his monarch's bosom. "*That man*," said the lovely pleader, " *is the wicked Haman*." Darting one look of vengeance on the petrified favorite, he strode forth into the garden to control his boiling passions. Haman saw at once that his only hope now was, in moving the sympathies of the queen in his behalf; and approaching her, he began to plead most piteously for his life. In his agony he fell on the couch where she lay, and while in this position, the king returned. 'What!' he exclaimed, 'will he violate the queen here in my own palace!' Nothing more was said: no order was given. The look and voice of terrible wrath in which this was said, were sufficient. The attendants simply spread a cloth over Haman's face, and not a word was spoken. Those who came in, when they saw the covered countenance, knew the import. It was the sentence of death. The vaunting favorite himself dare not remove it—he must *die*, and the quicker the agony is over, the better. In a few hours he was swinging on the gallows he had erected for Mordecai.

"After this, the queen's power was supreme—everything she asked was granted. To please her, he let his palace flow in the blood of five hundred of his subjects, whom the Jews slew in self-defence. For her he hung Haman's ten sons on the gallows where the father had suffered before them. For her he made Mordecai prime minister, and lavished boundless favors on the hitherto oppressed Hebrews. And right worthy was she of all he did for her. Lovely in character as she was in person, her sudden elevation did not make her vain, nor her power haughty. The same gentle, pure, and noble creature when queen, as when living in the lowly habitation of her cousin—generous, disinterested, and ready to die for others, she is one of the loveliest characters furnished in the annals of history."

After Esther, in the changing fortunes of Israel, till the Saviour's advent, but little reference is made to woman. The wife of Job, unsubdued by the terrible calamity that swept away her fortune and children, was his tempter in the darkest hour of his affliction. David, in his Psalms of surprising sweetness and sublimity, alludes to the virtues of "mothers in Israel"—and Solomon graphically delineates the character of the wife who "is from God." The prophets, in their lofty strains of prediction, and warning, and encouragement, make mention of her mission in coming scenes— her sufferings in national distress, when offspring shall clasp their parental knees in the agony of famine, "and pour out their souls in their mother's bosom." With rapture they follow her angel form in the rising glory of Zion—the mystery of redemption, and the approaching peace of millennial rest, when the harmonies of earth shall blend once more with the melodies of Heaven!

From the single promise that sent a ray of hope through the gloom of man's forsaken spirit in paradise, falling as the returning smile of God on nature reeling under his curse, to the last message of a dying prophet, the whole tide of events converged toward agr and consummation; a full manifestation of the grace which suspended the penalty of violated law. "God put forth his agencies, and calmly waited four thousand years for the accomplishment of his designs of mercy."

It was a faint spreading of dawn that cheered the pathway of Eve; but the increasing radiance gilded the horizon of Palestine, bathing the heights on which the seers bowed in rapture, till last of all Malachi poured forth his impassioned eloquence against Israel, and slept with his fathers.

Then followed four hundred years of trial and struggle; the people could only look back on the long track of wandering, rebuke and concentrating light pointing onward to a future whose shadows were lifting, and thus become able to bear the coming sun, and welcome its illumination.

Among those who were expecting a sublime manifestation of love in the advent of Messiah, was Zacharias, a venerable priest at Jerusalem, whose wife, a descendant of Aaron, was a woman of elevated piety.

They were now aged and childless. One evening as the fading light burnished the temple-columns, and streamed through the lofty windows upon the Mercy Seat, the Cherubim overshadowing it, and the golden altar, he passed thoughtfully through the multitude that crowded the gates of the sacred structure. His form disappeared in the Holy Place, and arrayed in his sacerdotal robes, he stood before the altar of incense, while the throng pressed into the porch to worship. Their prayer arose like the murmur of the ocean, but he was all alone by the flame of sacrifice, interceding for them. Suddenly he heard the rustling of wings, and on the oblation there came a glow more intense than the fire of his offering, and by his side he beheld an angel of the Lord in white apparel, with his face of celestial beauty beaming full upon him. He was troubled, and trembling with alarm would have shrunk away from the presence of Gabriel, but the tones of his gentle voice dispelled the rising fear, and he restored the calmness of faith. He listened with doubting surprise to the tidings, "Thy wife Elizabeth shall bear thee a son." Ah! he had prayed for the blessing in former years, and cherished the hope until it turned to ashes in his sad heart, while Elizabeth had made supplication till prayer seemed a mockery. He could not believe without a miraculous token, and this was added. But it was as though the offending lips were smitten by an unseen hand, for the angel left him *speechless*, and returned to the throne of God.

Zacharias turned away from the dying flame of his offering, and waving his hand to the people who had wondered at his long absence, went in silence to his dwelling. Elizabeth could not doubt the fulfilment of a promise which was expressed in tears and voiceless sighs, themselves a warning, not to limit the power of the Infinite One.

And then it was her pleasant employment to beguile the loneliness of her husband, who for her sake wore the seal of divine displeasure with cheerful piety, and affection which flowed with new and gathering strength in the deeper channel of maternal solicitude for a son connected with whose birth was "so exceeding great and precious promises."

But the scenes of that home are unrecorded, excepting a visit from her cousin Mary, the mother of Christ; an interview inexpressibly solemn and touching. The Holy Ghost was the companion of Elizabeth, and Mary carried a treasure which was the theme of ceaseless halleluiahs in Heaven. There was no jealousy, no glorying but in the Lord.

The salutation which welcomed the virgin indicates both humility of spirit and the strength of natural love; " And whence is it that the mother of my Lord should come to me?" Mary replied in a devotional rhapsody, to Him who " putteth down the mighty in their seats, and exalteth them of low degree." Three months were passed in delightful companionship. Their long conversations concerning " the consolation of Israel"—their hours of prayer around the domestic altar—their deep study of prophecy with the mute and subdued Zacharias, have no place in the memorials of earth; for none cared for these while transpiring in the " hill country of Juda."

The streets of Jerusalem echoed the tramp of Roman soldiery, and the haughty Pharisees swept the pavement with their phylactered robes of ceremonial sanctity. The busy world moved thoughtlessly on around these solitary women, while angels were on the wing for their protection, and if their safety required it, a chariot of fire would have descended to the green summits that girded the city. At length Mary sought again the retirement of her own habitation, and Elizabeth gave birth to a son. Amid the rejoicings of friends, the child was named Zacharias after his father. His mother insisted on calling him John, according to Gabriel's command. The matter was then referred to the aged and silent priest who was looking on; and he wrote with a stile on the waxen table, "He shall be called John." The people were amazed at this deviation from national custom. While gazing inquiringly upon him, his speech was restored, and he praised God until his humble dwelling seemed bursting with the swelling anthem. Then followed a burning strain of prophecy, running from the earliest predictions of Messiah, to the gathering of the Gentiles under his glory, mounting upward to "the rest which remains for the people of God."

The boyhood of John is mentioned no farther than that "he grew and waxed strong in spirit," but beneath his supernatural endowments and the greatness of his heraldic career, the maternal influence is clearly discernible in his lofty character. It is traceable as the waters of a stream by the lines of their coloring, long after they have entered the sea. We need no farther testimony that he neither had nor needed the angel of tradition to guard his early slumbers and guide his juvenile feet, than the saintly and gifted Elizabeth. He repeated the sentiments and nearly the language of that mother when he saw the majestic form of Jesus approaching him for baptism—"comest thou to me?" Her joy as a mother was lost in that of his sacred mission, as the Saviour's herald awakened; so John exclaimed when he saw and listened to Christ, "This my joy is fulfilled."

In all his ministry, it is beautifully manifest "that this 'burning and shining light' was kindled under the maternal wing at Hebron, as well as fanned into brilliancy by the wings of inspiration in the wilderness, that it might be a herald-star of the Sun of Righteousness."

GABRIEL figures so conspicuously in celestial vision, that the mind naturally takes the impression, he is a favorite angel in the embassage of Heaven to earth. He appeared twice to Daniel—talked with Zacharias while engaged in the temple service at evening, and not long afterward, "was sent from God to a city of Galilee, named Nazareth," to Mary. When he entered her lonely dwelling, he shouted in the transport of his own full heart, "Hail thou that art highly favored, the Lord is with thee: blessed art thou among women!" That bright form, and the startling salutation excited her fears, and she waited tremblingly for a farther disclosure. "Fear not, Mary," broke the silence and suspense of the scene, and in glowing language he announced to her the honor which could be given to but *one* woman in the universe—that of becoming the mother of "the Lord of Glory, the Prince of peace," in his humanity.

And here Mary forms a sublime contrast with Sarah and even the good old Zacharias, when visited by angels. There was no utterance of unbelief, no smile of incredulity, although there seemed to be an impossibility of fulfilment, without sinking hopelessly her reputation, and perhaps her untimely removal to a grave of infamy

For she was betrothed to Joseph, a worthy young man, and the appearance of infidelity would alienate him and expose her to the penalty of violated Law. Her sensitive spirit simply inquired, "How shall this be?" and Gabriel replied, "The Holy Ghost shall come upon thee, and the power of the Highest shall overshadow thee, and the holy thing which shall be born of thee shall be called the Son of God: For with God *nothing shall be impossible.*" All was yet folded in mystery—like one entering the "dark valley," she could lean alone on the Almighty, and walk trustingly under the cover of his wings.

Never in Heaven or in time, was there sweeter resignation—a more hopeful consecration amid unexplained difficulties, deep as human degradation, and wonders rising like vast shadows to the "clouds and darkness that environ the Throne." Fixing her gentle eye on the angel, she said, "Behold the handmaid of the Lord; be it unto me according to thy word." There was a solemn stillness of that maiden's heart, and a thrill of unutterable joy when the struggle was over, and she felt that her destiny was so nearly linked with the predicted Messiah. And as Gabriel departed from her for the skies, his last look toward the kneeling virgin, must have been full of tenderness and admiring love. We know not the interest and the high converse in glory as often as the messenger re-entered the unfolding gates, and repeated to the seraphim the story of his mission—then swept his lyre and sang "Alleluiah!" But what a murmur of wonder, and strange suspense passed over that throng, when their King laid down his sceptre, and his crown, and putting off the unsullied robes he had worn before a worshipper bowed at his feet, deserted the burning Throne for the form of Mary, and the helplessness of infancy in a world of enemies, and of gloom.

Mary was bewildered with the strange and crowding events of her hitherto quiet life in Nazareth, and turned her sympathy to her cousin Elizabeth, who was mature in holy experience, and, as the angel had said, soon to be the mother of Messiah's gifted herald—breaking the silence of centuries by the "voice of one crying in the wilderness, prepare ye the way of the Lord!" She received a joyful welcome—and the months passed on, to those humble dwellers in Hebron, with the solemn march of ages—for four thousand years flung their light and shadow upon them; they closed the long drama of preparation, and opened upon the world the glories of a new life, "and immortality."

And now came Joseph's trial. When he

perceived that Mary would be a mother, his first thought was to set aside the engagement, and leave her without exposure, to seclusion. But while hesitating amid the conflicting emotions exerted by his affection, which clung to apparently an unworthy object, and his honor involved in the result, Gabriel came to him in his restless slumbers and bade him dismiss his fears, and as a son of David, in accordance with prophecy, become the reputed father of Emanuel. Joseph arose from his repose, and with restored confidence and love, sought Mary and made her his wife.

Here the infidel may curl his impious lip, and in the affected majesty of reason and purity, lift his hand to blot out the hope of a weeping world; but not until *he* can stay the woful ravages of sin, hush the cry of the soul for a Redeemer, and offer rest to the weary and sorrowing, can he mantle with shame these touching miracles, that heralded the advent of "God manifest in the flesh."

"Actions are the glorious oratory of God!" and he speaks more eloquently and loudly in the incidents on which he hinges his designs, than in the roll of all his gathered thunders, or the roar of ocean rising in wrath at his whisper.

The Roman Emperor Augustus, *just at this time*, after a delay of twenty years, commanded that a census of the population of his vast empire be taken, and " each person be enrolled in the chief city of his family or tribe." This edict sent Mary and her husband to Bethlehem, the capital of the Davidic family.

Upon their arrival, the inns were full, and no place offered them but *a manger*, among the beasts of the stall. The night came down, and the hum of the little city ceased—the money-changers slept in their goodly dwellings, and even the shelterless found rest beneath the mild sky of Judea. Peace brooded over the earth from whose bosom contending armies had retired—the preparatory work was finished;—the still hour of midnight came on, and the friendless Mary gave birth to a SAVIOUR!

On the slopes of surrounding hills, shepherds kept the nightly watch of their folded flocks. They sat in musing mood, or gazing at the flashing spheres above, when the air grew luminous about them, and an Angel swept down the starry road in a flood of radiance that streamed from the opening sky, till the green pastures glowed like the very pavement of Heaven, and the faces of those watchers were white as marble, while they shook like Belteshazzar before the mystic hand that wrote his doom.

This angel, doubtless Gabriel, who said

to Mary, "Fear not," with the same language broke the silence, and with the "Good tidings of great joy" upon his lips, pointing to Bethlehem which lay in the shadow of distance, told the wandering shepherds they would "Find the babe wrapped in swaddling clothes, and lying in a manger." Then suddenly a multitude of the heavenly host thronged the illumined sky, and poured their melody along the hills until they took up the swelling anthem and sent it back to the "Eternal City," and then again with the new notes of gratulation the song of jubilee rolled down upon the brightening summits.

It is not strange, that the sinless choir who had sung together with "the morning stars" when the world hung in unmarred perfection, in the dawn of creation, and who walked in the beautiful garden—who held their harps in sadness when the frown of God darkened upon the sphere, he pronounced "very good," and his curse withered even the flowers upon its scathed and riven bosom, while the centuries wore away amid tears and blasphemy; that they should strain every string, and in their loftiest harmonies, lift the halleluiah "Glory to God in the highest, and on earth, peace and good will toward men."

Those glittering ranks returned to Paradise, and the melody died away on the ear of the shepherds hastening to Bethlehem. They bent adoringly over the child, and repeated the burden of that song. Mary, meditative and retiring, silently pondered the marvellous sayings that flew with the morning light from lip to lip of the gathering crowd. She named the infant JESUS, and according to the Mosaic ritual, passed the days of symbolical purification, and went up to the Temple with her sacrifice of turtle-doves

Here she found aged Simeon, waiting for "the consolation of Israel," and filled with the Holy Ghost, he took the babe in his arms, and raising his fading eyes toward Heaven he "blessed God, and said, Lord, now lettest thou thy servant depart in peace."

He spoke of the Saviour's mission in a higher sense than Joseph or Mary could understand, and turning to her, alluded to "the contradiction of sinners" that Son would endure, and to his fearful martyrdom, in words although dimly apprehended, that must have conveyed a mournful meaning to her anxious heart, "Yea a sword shall pierce through thy soul also." Anna, a prophetess eighty years old, also came in and joined Simeon in his devout ascription. And the infant Christ understood it all, and needing not the homage of men or of angels, he permitted Mary to caress him as fondly as ever a mother clasped the treasure of offspring to her breast. "One would like if he could, to lift the veil that hangs over the experience of Mary; and to learn of her who had the maternal care and guidance of the holy child Jesus; and to know what was the precise complexion of that moral dawn, which preceded the pure and perfect effulgence that shone forth on the history of his riper years; and to be told how richly all her tenderness was repaid, by smiles more lovely than ever before played on the infant countenance, and in his hours of anguish by such calm and unruffled serene as not one cry of impatience, and one moment of fretfulness, ever broke in upon."

During the stay at Bethlehem, the magi, led by a star, journeyed from the East to Jerusalem, inquiring for the Messiah, of whose predicted appearance they had heard from travelling Jews. Thence visiting the infant Saviour, they offered with their homage, the frankincense of Araby, and gifts of gold. Disregarding Herod's command to bring him word if Christ were found, they returned by another way. Herod, a sanguinary and heartless tyrant, was enraged at the insult, and commanded the slaughter of innocents, to destroy the future "King of the Jews." Oh! who can tell Mary's grief as their wail fell on her ear, and her agony of fear while flying from the dripping sword, to a strange land?

Upon the death of the royal infanticide, the hunted family retired again to Nazareth, their old place of residence. There Mary lived quietly, while Jesus grew up to youth, "waxing strong in spirit, and filled with wisdom." And who can doubt that in his humanity, under the training of so pure a mother, whose intellectual power was exhibited in her splendid *magnificat* when she met Elizabeth, he was regarded as a rare example of early piety, and that mother was the more admired and loved for the Son's sake. His manner always amiable—his language never breathing an unhallowed thought, or wayward impulse, or even the levity of juvenile pastimes, could not fail to impress his companions, and win their warmest affection, and the admiration of the Nazarines who frequented the lowly habitation of Joseph. When he was twelve years old, the family went, according to national custom, to the Holy City to keep the annual festival of the Passover. They worshipped with wonted solemnity, and offered their oblations.

Returning in company with others to their own country, they had journeyed all day from Jerusalem without missing the Saviour, who unobserved went back to the Temple. The parents were troubled, and hastened to seek for the lost one in the streets of the crowded city. After three days of fruitless effort, at last they entered the consecrated edifice, where lingered the proud Pharisee, and the strangers who came to admire the splendid sanctuary of the Most High. And there, in the midst of venerable doctors, with the open Law and Prophets before them, sat Jesus, silencing their wise interpretations, by his greater wisdom. The sight amazed his weary and anxious parents, to whom there evidently seemed a change in his docile nature, distinguished for obedience, which ever before anticipated their request. There is a tone of rebuke in Mary's questioning, which has all the fulness of a mother's love—"Son, why hast thou thus dealt with us? behold thy father and I have sought thee sorrowing." His reply was the first hint of Divine commission and Deity to them—"Wist ye not that I must go about *my Father's* business?" This was above their comprehension, for they had regarded him simply as Messiah—appointed by Jehovah, and committed to their care for the deliverance from Roman dominion, of their captive nation.

But Mary was deeply and devoutly contemplative. Jesus went with them to Nazareth, and was again a beautiful example of subjection, while she dwelt in earnest thought, upon the import of his words, and the God-like spirituality of his life. In the maturity of youth, he entered on his work, but did not forget his mother. And soon after, we find them with the disciples at a marriage festival in Cana, where the Saviour evidently mingled with his friends in the cheerful intercourse of such an occasion.

From some oversight or want of means, there was no wine for the guests. Mary had witnessed miracles enough to know his word could supply them—and calling him aside, suggested the exercise of his power. His answer to the superficial readers of the narration seems harsh—" Woman, what have I to do with thee, mine hour is not yet come." But the form of address was common, and perfectly respectful. It is as if he had said, while his beaming eye and benign countenance were eloquent with affection, " Mother, why anticipate and direct in my designs—I know my mission and every step of its fulfilment." Mary evidently became weary of travel in following her Son, and would have him retire from his public activity; for while he was in the synagogue at Capernaum, she waited at the door, while a messenger called him. The result of the entreaty is not recorded, but he tenderly employed the incident to express his higher and living union with his people—that relation which should abide, when human associations have vanished, and "earth, like a pebble, is sunk in the ocean of a past eternity."

She was in the train that accompanied the Saviour to Jerusalem, before his martyrdom—but all unconscious of the weight of sorrow under which his mighty heart was sinking.

We do not know where she was when the stars looked down upon his wrestling in Gethsemane, while the crimson dew of his agony started from every pore—when he received unresistingly the traitor's kiss, and high-priest's buffeting—when in the hall, where justice was a mockery, and insult the sentence of condemnation—and when he bore up the rugged summit the instrument of torture, till crushed by its weight—but we find that mother beside the Cross, while the warm blood was gushing from the sacred form she cradled in infancy, and without a cheering voice, he trod the wine-press of his Father's wrath. She beheld the drooping head—the brow wrung with anguish, and the quivering lips. She listened to the cry, while hell was in suspense, and Heaven bent with wonder over the scene, "My God! My God! why hast thou forsaken me?"

Mary could offer no relief, and her maternal solicitude would not permit a withdrawal from the Mount of Crucifixion. Oh! the suffering of that loving spirit, when not only her Son was expiring in unutterable agonies, but the hope of his followers, was going out in rayless midnight. By her side was the youthful John, sympathizing with his Master, and weeping with Mary. The eye of the Sufferer, though the penalty of eternal Law was tearing its way through his sinless bosom, and he sustained alone a world's redemption, rested upon her he loved before he took up his abode with her; and pointing to John, he said with dying affection, "Woman, behold thy Son!"

Those accents and that last look expressed it all. It was saying amid the throes of agony unknown to man, "My mother, I must leave you, but he shall cheer your mournful years—give him my place as son, in your holy love." Turning to the Beloved Disciple, he said, "Behold thy mother!" It would seem from the words "that very hour," that John immediately obeyed, and induced her to leave the scene of deepening and accumulating horrors.

Who could fathom her grief when she heard of that death amid taunts and sneers, the rocking earth and blackening skies; and finally of his unattended burial. And oh! how her drooping spirit smiled out through tears of joy, when the news of his resurrection spread, and once more she beheld the immaculate Jesus!

We next hear of Mary when returning from Mount Olivet, from whose shining top the Saviour ascended to the Throne of his Glory in a chariot of cloud, the disciples joined the circle of prayer in the "upper room" at Jerusalem. She was there before the Mercy Seat, drawn thither by the clearer rays of Divinity from the *Son of God*, that taught her how to pray.

That Mary was a maiden of remarkable loveliness, is inferable from her selection by Jehovah as the mother of his "Only-begotten and well-beloved Son." Her maternal character is without a blemish;—"Blessed art thou among women!" is the epitaph every devout heart would inscribe on her tomb.

MARTHA.

TURNING from the scenes and biography of the Old Dispensation to those of the New, is like going from a planet where moonlight only brightened on the landscape, forest and flood; where mysterious shadows swept along the rustling woods of the mountain-side, and strange voices haunted the air, and where even the noblest characters were invested with a romantic interest; to a sphere where the glad light of morning floods the plains, and the clear accents of truth and hope greet the ear, while rejoicing woman leaning on the beating heart of man, her brow calm and beautiful in the dignity of a faith which looks steadily into the portal of a better life, breathes a sympathy warm and gushing for the sorrows of a common humanity.

Christ poured this new effulgence on the paths of men, and taught a philanthropy expansive as his own infinite benevolence. The Divinity of the Redeemer was veiled in a nature that could sympathize with all that was lovely, tender, joyous, or mournful, in the fallen ones he came to save. Though sinless, he was a man of sorrows, and found those in the circle of his followers, with whom he enjoyed that near attachment, and familiar interchange of thought and feeling peculiar to the intimacies and fellowship of kindred spirits.

The family of Bethany—Martha, Mary, and Lazarus, an only brother, were among those cherished friends of the Saviour.—They were evidently orphans, and all deeply devout. He often sat at their table, and communed with them in the unchecked gushings of his great and oft over-burdened heart. While pursuing his ministry in the region about Jerusalem, not unfrequently after the toil and travel of the day, the scorn of enemies, and misunderstanding of doubting disciples, he sought this peaceful home, to refresh his drooping spirit with the cheering cordialities of friendship, pure as it was changeless. There, looking upon Olivet, in whose solemn shades he was wont to pray, and with doomed Salem, whose far-off murmur was heard by him, pressing upon his soul, he sat at the twilight hour, while they washed his weary feet, and bathed his throbbing temples. And then with an eye radiant as a star, and a smile of unearthly sweetness, he discoursed to them of his works of mercy, and his glorious kingdom, destined to restore to earth her primal blessedness and peace.

It was well they had not a full disclosure of his ineffable majesty, for they could not in their awful reverence, have admitted him into all the secrecies of personal regard, and leaned on his breast in unshrinking trust. Oh! what a guest was Immanuel! The Wonderful, the Counsellor—the Almighty, bestowing the fulness of his love on the creatures of his power, and opening to them the depths of his heart.

The first domestic scene narrated, illustrates the contrast of character in the two sisters. The Saviour had accepted the invitation of the elder sister, Martha, to become an inmate of their humble dwelling. She was active aud impulsive, making haste to spread a repast worthy of her Lord. Mary, thoughtful and inquiring, sat at the feet of Christ to hear his "gracious words," forgetful of the domestic duties which absorbed Martha's attention. She was of calmer temperament, and would have made a recluse of elevated, devotional spirit—one of that saintly few, whose souls are "as when the waters of a lake are suffered to deposit their feculence, and to become as pure as the ether itself; so that they not only reflect from their surface the splendor of Heaven, but allow the curious eye to gaze delighted upon the decorated grottos and sparkling caverns of the depth beneath."

She was riveted to her seat by the accent of Him who "spake as never man spake." Martha was touched by this neglect, and in her sudden irritation, reproached Jesus for permitting her to cast the entire burden of household cares upon another. Oh! there is the mildness and majesty of a God in the kind reproof:—" Martha, Martha, thou art careful and troubled about many things; but one thing is needful; and Mary hath chosen that good part which shall not be taken from her."

But that domestic group soon after passed under the cloud of affliction. The brother, their dependence and constant companion, was smitten down by disease, and wasting before its ravages, while Jesus was far away preaching to the multitudes of Bethabara. Therefore the sisters sent unto him saying: "Lord, behold he whom *thou lovest* is sick."

Though he knew it all before the messenger came, and was a deeply interested spectator of that distant chamber of suffering, he did not hasten hither, but tarried two days longer. In this way he always answers prayer—he takes his own time, and though he may seem to disappoint, he sends the blessing just when it will accomplish the highest good for the petitioner, and advance his own glory. Accompanied by his disciples, who marvelled at his strange language concerning the now departed Lazarus, for whose sake he was about to expose himself to the rage of his foes, the Saviour journeyed toward Bethany. Soon as Martha heard of his approach, she went forth in her tears to meet him, while Mary in her excessive grief, sat in the desolate dwelling, unconscious of passing scenes, and unheeding the footsteps of those who came to fling a ray of comfort athwart the gloom of bereavement.

In this touching incident, is again developed the differing shades of character in these lovely maidens. The quiet earnestness of Mary, makes her a mourner of inapproachable and sublime sorrow—like a monument, solemn and voiceless, bearing only the inscription of the dead on its breast. She was one who felt that

> "With *silence* only as their benediction,
> God's angels come
> Where in the shadow of a great affliction
> The soul sits dumb!"

But Martha, with hurried step, sought the highway Jesus was travelling, and looking into his placid face, with the commingling emotions of sorrow over blasted hope and unabated affection, she said, "If thou hadst been here, my brother had not died." He replied with a tone of authority, "Thy brother shall rise again." Doubtful of the import of this calm assurance, yet confiding in his power, she hastened to call the disconsolate Mary. At the mention of his name, she also ran to embrace him, and in the tones of bleeding love, used the same language of disappointment which just before stirred the soul of her returning Lord.

The crowd who had gathered to extend their condolence, thought the mourners had gone to the tomb to weep in solitude, and they followed in the distance; for their sympathies had become excited, and tears fell like rain. When Jesus beheld the scene of lamentation, "He groaned in spirit and was troubled." Oh! what internal agitation was there—how that bosom in which the faintest shadow of sin had never dimmed the unsullied light of moral excellence, was tossed with emotion, and what a "mastery of love" found utterance; when he said, "*Where have ye laid him?*" "Lord, come and see," was the hopeful reply, as they turned in their grief to the sepulchre, which enshrined the decaying form of Lazarus. Bending over it, "Jesus wept." The Jews marvelled at his strong love for the sleeper, while he lifted his fervent prayer. Then, with a voice so loud it rang through the hopeless chamber of death, and over the bright tops of the celestial hills, he cried, "Lazarus, come forth!" and the motionless heart grew warm and stirred, the color mantled the bandaged cheek, and the light of a living soul was rekindled beneath the parted lids! The buried friend of Christ again beheld Him, and loosed from the habiliments of the grave, greeted with wonted tenderness, the astonished yet joyful sisters.

The gratitude, the raptures, and frequent interviews with the Son of God which followed, are lost with the countless words of wisdom, and acts of mercy in the unwritten history of Him who wasted no moments, and neglected no sufferer that crossed his path.

A few days before the last passover, the Saviour went again to Bethany, with a company of disciples. The family on which he seemed to lavish his love and confidence, gave him a supper. Lazarus sat by his side, while Martha, with characteristic vivacity, and generous hospitality, prepared the feast; but Mary in her own beautiful sensibility, and depth of feeling, noiseless as the tide that lies tranquilly in its unsounded caves, was reclining by the feet of Jesus. She poured upon them precious ointment, till the perfume filled the apartment, and wiped those sacred limbs with the flowing ringlets of her raven hair.

It was the occasion of bringing out the sordid and selfish spirit of Judas, who complained of Mary's extravagance. The unrelenting malignity of his open enemies was also awakened by the presence of the brother, He had recalled from the realm of the dead. Oh! who can doubt the truthfulness of this simple story, when at no point can we pause and say, *nature* is not here; or who can question the strength and madness of that depravity which could invade the sweet solemnities of such a scene?

It was the last visit of the Redeemer to Bethany—that anointing was for his burial—and he went to the "City of his tears," to be the martyr of a world—and a spectacle of wonder to the universe he made, and which a breath of his power could sweep away like the gossamer web woven in the dew of morning.

Among the many lessons of this biography, no one is more impressive than the law of kindness and charity, seen in all the narrative and enforced by the rebuke of Christ to Martha. She was a christian, ever active, and prompt to do the external duties of religion. Because Mary was of a different temperament, and more retiring, she judged her harshly, and the Redeemer who would not send her away from his feet.

And so it often happens that a Godly

person, uniform and serious in character, will condemn another whose animal spirits as naturally run high, and whose impulses are like the rushing wave. There is no apology for a sacrifice of *principle*—but let none sit self-complacently in judgment upon a fellow-worm, when God by his forming hand, has emphatically " made them to differ"—but learn of Him who was meek and lowly of heart, by a frown of displeasure or a cruel word, never to " break the bruised reed, or quench the smoking flax ;" for life is formed of *trifles*, and their imperishable influence and value, will appear in the grand summing up of the final Judgment.

XIX
DORCAS.

CHRIST ascended from Olivet, the Mount of his prayer, and with uplifted hands left upon the disciples who gazed after his loved and vanishing form, a benediction perpetual as his militant church. They went forth in the stern heroism of primitive apostleship through the valleys of Judea, and to the cities that dotted them, and gemmed the shores of distant seas.

Among these beacon-points of the Gospel,

was Joppa, or anciently Yaffa, on a promontory of the Mediterranean coast, forty miles from Jerusalem. It was an ancient city, associated with the names of Æolus, and Andromeda of classical fiction—it is mentioned by Joshua, and was the port to which the cedars of Lebanon and treasures of kings were floated for the first and second Temples of the Holy City. Here Jonah embarked when he thought "on the wings of the morning," to flee from the hand of God. Juda Maccabeus, to avenge a broken treaty, drove two hundred Jews from its heights into the sea, and made a conflagration of the shipping, that like an opening volcano, illumined the wide grave that swept over them. And even Napoleon's legions in later time thundered before its gates.

But all these events recede into the dimness of eclipse, around the scenes which have transpired in the dwelling of Tabitha, and which shall survive the cenotaphs of royal heroes as they successively moulder, written in the history and blending with the converse of Heaven.

She was a pious woman, and distinguished especially for an expansive and active benevolence—a deep and genial sympathy for the " fatherless and the widow in their affliction." She may have been bereft of a husband, and in the sad discipline of domestic calamities prepared for that sublimest effort of an immortal, doing good in a world where the funeral knell never ceases to roll its fearful cadence on the reluctant ear of the living, and tears fall more constantly than the nightly dew—and where hearts are breaking, and spiritual victories gained and battles lost, invested with an interest compared with which, a falling throne and vanishing empire, are no more than the shivered toy and bursting bauble on the playground of childhood. Or she may have preferred like Hannah, of recent memory, the disencumbered activity of single life, and stood in vestal loveliness beside the altar of devotion to her risen Redeemer, whose voice of love seemed yet to linger in the air of Palestine.

Whatever her condition, it is enough to know that she bent all her energies to imitate the faultless model of philanthropy, and extend the glory of His name by illustrating the transcendent excellence of christian character.

But in the midst of usefulness, death calls for the saint. It could not be otherwise than that she marked his approach with a smile, and went down untremblingly into the valley of gloom. The corpse was laid out in "an upper chamber," and from the hovels of the poor, and dwellings of the rich, came the mourners to weep together, and look once more on the face it had been so pleasant to meet when upon her errands of mercy. Their thoughts turned to Peter, whose faith and intellectual energy won confidence, and maintained an influence unquestioned, among the disciples of Jesus.

Two messengers hastened to Lydda, informed him of their irreparable loss, and requested him, without delay, to return with them to the house of mourning. When Peter entered the room, and saw the weeping widows Tabitha had comforted and clothed, encircling the dead, and also the garments she had made for the destitute; impressed by the spirit, he felt that her work was not done—the struggling church could not spare the shining light.

He sent the unwilling group from the apartment in wondering silence, and knelt by the pale sleeper. It was not needful that his petition should be long, for it was the "fervent, effectual prayer of the righteous man." Then looking upon the marble brow, he said, "Tabitha, arise!" The eye opened with its wonted lustre, and when she saw the noble apostle, she began to rise. Peter extended his hand, and calling to "the saints and widows," presented her again to their cordial greeting, while the news spread through the streets of Joppa. The skeptical were convinced, and many who had scorned the Nazarene, were added to the number of true believers.

In Scripture, there is a uniform simplicity and beauty, which dwells upon no scene however inviting, if unimportant to the great design of Revelation. Mystery rests on the interval between the death and resurrection of those restored to life—upon the inquiry whether they brought any tidings from the unseen land, and their final departure from earth.

In reviewing the sacred annals of the past, we find that woman has often laid her hand on the springs of a world's destiny, coiled in decisive events; and from her sanctified genius, have streamed the radiating lines of redeeming influence over the world. But it is in the circle of *home*, she puts forth a power exceeding all other human agency. As a maiden, she can elevate and refine a brother, or strengthen upon him a taste for exciting pleasures, which shall hurry him away from the moorings of manly principle and promise, into the broad sweep of the current which descends at length into the abyss of moral ruin in time, blending its roar with the dash of those billows which have no shore, and whose shipwrecked victims find no oblivious grave. In the social relation, results are the same.

As a wife, it is her's to make the domestic scene attractive and benign in its influence upon him whose happiness, and often destiny forever, is at her disposal under God. They are in one bark on the sea of life—and though he may be unskillful or erring, and sink her treasure of hope and joy, yet if she be true and holy, the barge will founder long before it goes darkly down, and she will disappear with the wreck like an angel of the troubled waters, to rise again with a martyr's wreath, and a song of victory.

As a mother, she leaves the moulding impress of her hand on her offspring, as the potter on the clay, he shapes to honor or dishonor. A pious and consistent mother *always* in the final issue has her reward. Nowhere does the terrific law, " as a man soweth, so shall he also reap," come in with more certain consequences than in this relation. She may breathe her hallowed counsel in a reluctant ear—baptize a brow of shame with her tears, and lift her prayer with breaking heart over the couch of the thoughtless sleeper; but around that son, is flung a spell the song of revelry and the shout of blasphemy can never break. He will be haunted through the thousand-pathed labyrinth of sin, with an invisible presence, before whose gentle accents and heavenly face he will bow and weep. And though she go to the grave mourning for the wanderer, he shall come to the green mound in after life and make it the shrine of penitence and altar of consecration to God.

And silently as the morning light, her influence goes forth everywhere; as it once marred, so is it to be mighty in restoring the glorious image of the Deity to man.

———" Oh! if now,
Woman would lift her noble wand she bore
In Paradise so transcendent, and which still she wears
Half-hidden though not powerless, and again
Wave its magic power o'er pilgrim man,
How would she win him from apostasy,
Lure back the world from its dim path of woe,
And open a new Eden on our years."

BOOKS RECENTLY PUBLISHED BY DERBY & MILLER.

The Young Man's Book: or Lectures for the Times. By William W. Patton. One 12mo. vol.

The lectures contained in this volume are not made up of merely common place remarks. They are elevated in sentiment, chaste in style, and impressive in manner. No person who reads the volume can fail to profit by it, or to admire the evangelical views and elegant language of the author. The work deserves to be a favorite with young men.—*Northern Christian Advocate.*

It is a genial, earnest, manly book. The author is himself a remarkable example of independent thinking and philanthropic feeling. The bugle note which he sounds to young men is no uncertain sound. He goes with his whole soul for bettering the world, where he thinks it bad, and few of the young men who heard his lectures or shall read his book, will not be strongly inclined to go with him. We cordially advise all young men who are anxious to *do* and *be* something in this universe, to cultivate an acquaintance with Mr. Patton or his book.—*Boston Chronotype.*

There are seven lectures in this volume devoted to subjects rather unusual in a work of this kind, and having the impress of earnest feeling and reflection. That some of the points are overstated does not detract from the exceeding value and importance of most of the views presented—all the more important because so infrequently attended to in the pulpit, or in works designed for the young. The book is written in a perspicuous and forcible style, and both from its matter and spirit is likely to become popular and useful.—*New York Evangelist.*

This is an excellent book—excellent in its purpose, in its execution, and in its adaptation to the present day. In some respects this book differs from all kindred works that we have seen. As a writer Mr. Patton is lucid, earnest, and direct, never obscure and seldom other than forcible. Regarded merely as a literary performance we must pronounce these lectures highly creditable. Their timely and important moral inculcations should commend them more especially to the friends of religion and entitle them to a place in every christian household.—*Charter Oak.*

These are able and earnest lectures to young men, delivered to the author's congregation in Hartford, and contain many valuable considerations and glowing appeals to rouse the youth to diligence, courage, and faith in the struggle of life.—*New York Observer.*

The counsels, warnings, and encouragements, to the young, contained in this volume, are, as designed, adapted to the times. It is interesting in its style as well as matter, and cannot fail to profit that class to whom it is addressed.—*The (Boston) Puritan.*

The author of these lectures is himself a young man. He has addressed those of his own age, not with the stern reproof or grave counsel of a father, but with the affectionate entreaty, kind, yet faithful warning of a brother. The subjects of the lectures are judiciously selected and cannot fail of doing good to those who are soon to bear the burdens and responsibilities of society.—*Boston Recorder.*

A volume of lectures, seven in number, on subjects of vast importance, and written with much force. The book will profit those who read it.—*New York Commercial Advertiser.*

The lectures were delivered on Sabbath evenings to densely crowded audiences, and were spoken of in terms of high praise at the time. At the request of many who heard them they are now published. The lectures are valuable, containing a vast amount of good advice and information for that class of persons for whom they were originally designed, and in a time like the present, when pernicious literature appears to be the order of the day, they are still more acceptable.—(*Hartford*) *Christian Secretary.*

We can positively say that the object of the work is most praiseworthy, the subjects treated of are important, the counsels it contains are weighty, and are enforced in a happy style with a spirit well calculated to gain the attention of those who are addressed.—*Hartford (Ct.) Courant.*

In design and execution it is worthy to go side by side with the late popular and widely circulated work known as Beecher's Lectures to Young Men. The fifth lecture is well suited to our columns and we hope to give it a place ere long.—*N. Y. Advocate and Family Guardian.*

BOOKS RECENTLY PUBLISHED BY DERBY & MILLER.

Golden Steps to Respectability, Usefulness and Happiness;
being a series of Lectures to the youth of both sexes on Character, Principles, Associates, Amusements, Religion, and Marriage. By JOHN MATHER AUSTIN. Derby, Miller & Co., Auburn, 1850. 243 pp.

The author of this book is a writer of superior attraction, and has here selected a subject of deep interest. Could the youth of the country be induced to exchange the Buntline, Lippard, and Ingraham literature of the day, for such reading as this, the benefits to themselves and society would be incalculable.—*Lockport Courier.*

We honor the heart of the writer of this volume as well as his head. He has here addressed an earnest and manly appeal to the young, every page of which proves his sincerity and his desire for their welfare. The subjects treated of in the different lectures are those indicated on the title page. Integrity and virtue, usefulness, truth and honor, are the "Golden Steps" by which the young may ascend to respectability, usefulness, and happiness. We trust the seed thus sown will not be without its fruit, and that his readers will imbibe the spirit of the motto he has chosen—

"Onward! onward! toils despising,
Upward! upward! turn thine eyes,
Only be content when rising,
Fix thy goal amid the skies."
—*Albany State Register.*

The work of Mr. Austin, written in a pleasing style, and nervous and pointed in its argumentation, will hold a prominent position among the fortunate endeavors by which the rising generation are to be influenced. The volume before us is beautiful in its exterior, and this, combined with the aim of the author, in which he has admirably succeeded, will give it a wide range, and secure for it, we hope, an invaluable influence.—*Buffalo Christian Advocate.*

A plain, familiar, forcible exposition of the duties and responsibilities of Youth, which can hardly be read without exerting a salutary and lasting influence. Judging from the popularity of Mr. Austin's former works, we predict for it a wide circulation.—*New York Tribune.*

If the precepts eloquently and forcibly urged in these pages could be brought home and impressed upon the minds of the mass of youth in our land, they would confer lasting and incalculable benefits upon the rising generation. We cordially commend this work to the attention of the young and all who have charge of them.

The publishers have executed their work admirable, and have brought out an elegant and beautiful book. Their work will compare favorably with any of the New York houses.—*Troy Post.*

The following extract has reference to the "golden steps" of the President of th United States, Millard Fillmore :—(See page 69.)

BOOKS RECENTLY PUBLISHED BY DERBY & MILLER.

The Lives of Mary and Martha, mother and wife of Washington: by Margaret C. Conkling, with a steel portrait, 18mo, scarlet cloth.

MISS CONKLING, who is a daughter of Judge Conkling of Auburn, is favorably known as the author of Harper's translation of "Florian's History of the Moors of Spain." She also wrote "Isabel, or the Trials of the Heart." In the preparation of the pretty little volume she has done a praiseworthy deed, and we hope she will receive the reward she merits. She has taught us in the work

"how divine a thing
A woman may be made."

The mother and wife of Washington were, in many respects, model women, and the daughters of America will do well to study their character — which is finely drawn on these pages.— *Literary Messenger.*

This beautifully printed and elegantly bound little work, reflecting the highest credit upon the skill and task of the publishers, contains biographical sketches of Mary, the mother, and Martha, the wife of the Father of his country. It is a most valuable contribution to the history of the American people, embracing not only the great public events of the century during which the subjects lived, but those pictures of home life, and that exhibition of social manners and customs, which constitute the most important part of life, but which, from the fact of their apparent triviality and intangibility, the historian generally passes over. The authoress evidently sympathises earnestly with her subject, and feels that in the exhibition of those womanly virtues which characterized the heroines of her narrative, she makes the most eloquent plea in favor of the dignity of her sex. It is dedicated to Mrs. WM. H. SEWARD, and contains a finely executed engraving of the wife of Washington. We cordially commend it to the public, and most especially our lady readers.— *Syracuse Journal.*

This acceptable and well written volume goes forth upon a happy mission,

"To teach us how divine a thing
A woman may be made,"

by unfolding those charms of character which belong to the mother and wife of the hero of the Land of the Free; and in the companionship of which, while they illustrated the watchful tenderness of a mother, and the confiding affections of a wife, is shown those influences which made up the moral sentiments of a man, whose moral grandeur will be felt in all that is future in government or divine in philosophy; and one whose name is adored by all nations, as the leader of man in in the progress of government, to that perfection of human rights where all enjoy liberty and equality. To say that Miss Conkling has fulfilled the task she says a "too partial friendship has assigned her" faultlessly, would perhaps be too unmeasured praise, for perfection is seldom attained; but it will not be denied but that her biographies are traced in the chaste elegances that belong to the finished periods of a refined style, which fascinates the reader with what she has thus contributed to our national literature.

The design of the volume is, to picture a *mother* fitting the "Father of his Country," in a light full of the inexhaustible nobleness of woman's nature, and yet as possessing that subdued and quiet simplicity, where Truth becomes the Hope on which Faith looks at the future with a smile. The mother of Washington was tried in a school of practice where frugal habits and active industry were combined with the proverbial excellences of those Virginia matrons, who were worthy mothers of such men as Washington, Jefferson, Marshall, and Henry. Miss C. has pictured with fidelity and elegance, her views of this remarkable woman; not less beautifully has she sketched the character of Martha, the wife; following her from her brilliant manners as the Virginia belle, through the various phases of her life, she gives a rapid but comprehensive view of those characteristics which make up the quiet refinement of manners native to her, and which ever gave her the reputation of an accomplished wife and lady. And with peculiar delicacy Miss Conkling has portrayed the thousand virtues with which she embellished a home; her amiable disposition and winning manners made the happiest to the purest and best of all men fame has chosen for its noblest achievments.— *Syracuse Star.*

BOOKS RECENTLY PUBLISHED BY DERBY & MILLER.

The Missionary Offering, a memorial of Christ's Messengers in Heathen Lands, dedicated to Dr. Judson, 8 engravings, 12mo., muslin. $1,25.

We have seen no book of late which, upon a hasty examination, we could more cheerfully and confidently recommend. The history of the labors of Missionaries in foreign lands has always been one of unsurpassed interest to a great class of every community, by whom such enterprizes are conducted, and in no similar work have we seen this history more ably and truthfully set forth than in the one before us.— *Buffalo Commercial Advertiser.*

Here is a volume of about four hundred pages, neatly printed and illustrated, made up of the most interesting matter, from the pens of the first writers. Such a work cannot fail to interest. What a glorious band have cast aside the heart-clinging ties of home, country, and friends, and borne the peaceful emblem of Christianity to the darkest climes. Bloody rites have ceased, the funeral flame is extinguished, the crushing car has ceased to roll, and mental and moral darkness has given away before the silent labors of the missionary. The records of such a history cannot but interest, revealing as they do, some of the sublimest features in the character of man — sacrifices and toils and triumphs, before which the brightest achievements of earth dwindle into folly.— *Cayuga Chief.*

THE MISSIONARY OFFERING is composed of poetical and prose writings of rare excellence, reminiscences and incidents connected with foreign and home missions, &c. We consider it a valuable and interesting book, especially to the Christian and philanthropist, and all who look upon the missionary enterprise as an institution, under the guidance of Providence, for the moral regeneration of the world.—*Geneva Gazette.*

Rational Psychology, or the subjective idea and the objective law of all intelligence: by Laurens P. Hickok, D. D., Professor of Christian Theology in the Theological Seminary, Auburn.

The few, not the many, will find pleasure and improvement in the study of a treatise like this, discussing with much ability and research, indicative of close and patient thought, the abstruse science of mind, and reaching principles by a careful induction of well arranged and considered facts. The author has favorably introduced himself, in this work, to the thinking portion of the religious public, and will calmly await the verdict of the learned world upon this elaborate performance. It is a handsomely printed octavo of 700 pages.— *N. Y. Observer.*